THE FRUIT OF THE SPIRIT

THE MEASURE OF CHRISTIAN MATURITY

ANDY RIPLEY

THE SOURCE MINISTRIES

CONTENTS

1 THE CONTEXT

As we begin to study the fruit of the Spirit, I think it is good for us to take note of the context in which we find the fruit of the Spirit being spelled out for us. And, of course, the bigger context is the entire letter to the Galatians, which was written by Paul in response to a growing problem in the church. The problem was that some false teachers were luring the Galatians into a distorted gospel where works of the flesh were necessary in order to gain justification. The false teachers were convincing the Galatians that they had to become Jewish before they could become Christians – requiring gentile believers to be circumcised. This in effect was creating a mindset where the believers thought they were bringing about their own justification through the works which they did. Paul said that this was a completely different gospel than the gospel that he had preached to them, where justification came solely through faith in Jesus Christ. So, the bigger context where we discover the fruit of the Spirit being presented is in a framework comparing what is different about what your own works can produce and what the Holy Spirit can produce in you.

Zooming in on chapter five of Galatians we see the same context in concentrated form. So instead of just reading a couple of verses about the fruit, we should read a bit more of the surrounding passage. Not reading the entire book, but ten verses which will be able to give us a pretty good look at the bigger picture – as well as a close-up of some important individual issues.

Galatians 5:16-25   But I say, walk by the Spirit, and you will not gratify the desires of the flesh. 17 For the desires of the flesh are against the Spirit, and the desires of the Spirit are against the flesh, for these are opposed to each other, to keep you from doing the things you want to do. 18 But if you are led by the Spirit, you are not under the law. 19 Now the works of the flesh are evident: sexual immorality, impurity, sensuality, 20 idolatry, sorcery, enmity, strife, jealousy, fits of anger, rivalries, dissensions, divisions, 21 envy, drunkenness, orgies, and things like these. I warn you, as I warned you before, that those who do such things will not inherit the kingdom of God. 22 But the fruit of the Spirit is love, joy, peace, patience, kindness, goodness, faithfulness, 23 gentleness, self-control; against such things there is no law. 24 And those who belong to Christ Jesus have crucified the flesh with its passions and desires. 25 If we live by the Spirit, let us also keep in step with the Spirit.

When Paul introduces the fruit of the Spirit in Galatians 5:22, he does not say fruits of the Spirit, but fruit (singular). Many have taken this to mean that there is only one true fruit of the Spirit. Some say that all these virtues added together make up the fruit of the Spirit. Others say that the fruit is really the first one in the list, love, and the rest of the list are just differing ways to express or demonstrate love. And we can see several of these virtues used in this way in I Corinthians 13, where they are tied to love. Love is patient, and love is kind, for example. Still others point out that fruit in the singular can also be used in the plural just like in English. In other words, fruit can be used for fruits. You can say, "I like fruit." And that singular use of the word can have a plural meaning. When you say "I like fruit" it means you like grapes, you like apples, you like oranges, etc. So, the singular use of the word can have a plural meaning, making these virtues into the fruits of the Spirit. And also, some, with more language expertise than me, say that grammatically these verses read like a list of qualities of equal status. Often when we find lists of things in the Bible, scholars and theologians tell us that they are listed in order of importance, from first to last. But some say that this list is an exception. Meaning that they all have independent, equal meaning for us.

In verse sixteen above, Paul talks about walking by the Spirit. In verse eighteen, we hear of being led by the Spirit. In verse twenty-four we are among those who belong to Jesus Christ. And in verse twenty-five, we are encouraged that if we indeed live in the Spirit, then we ought to keep in step with the Spirit. All of these are descriptions of what it means to be a true Christian. So, first of all we are talking about living the Christian life. Those who walk by the Spirit, those who are led by the Spirit, those who belong to Jesus, those who are living by the Spirit; who are they? They are Christians. So, the fruit of the Spirit is then the character traits, the attitudes, and the attributes of the Christian person. The fruit of the Spirit is the imitation of Jesus Christ. Living a life that expresses and demonstrates the fruit of the Spirit is not for a special few people, it is for all of us who belong to Jesus. Living this kind of life is the expected Christian normal.

Another thing to notice in the context here is that walking by the Spirit creates a conflict. There is opposition to walking this way. And the primary opposition is not from Satan, but is from within ourselves. The opposition to living such a life comes primarily from the flesh. Verse seventeen says, "For the desires of the flesh are against the Spirit, and the desires of the Spirit are against the flesh, for these are opposed to each other, to keep you from doing the things you want to do." To live this Christian life is a battle, it's a war. It takes a little bit of fight from us to do it. It takes a bit of resistance to the desires of the flesh. Which necessarily means then, that it takes **from us** some resistance **to us.**

Verse twenty-four tells us that those who belong to Jesus Christ have crucified the flesh with its passions and desires. As Christians, as people of the cross, we crucify our own flesh with its passions and desires. Those who belong to Jesus Christ are people who deny themselves, take up their cross and follow Him. Those who belong to Jesus Christ are people who have the strange habit of opposing their own flesh, of fighting against their own fleshly tendencies. So, there is a kind of spiritual warfare for us to fight; which is not primarily against the devil. We necessarily go to war against our own flesh because we cannot remain as we used to be and be able to represent the Lord as His sent ambassadors.

Galatians 5:19-21   Now the works of the flesh are evident: sexual immorality, impurity, sensuality, 20 idolatry, sorcery, enmity, strife, jealousy, fits of anger, rivalries, dissensions, divisions, 21 envy, drunkenness, orgies, and things like these. I warn you, as I warned you before, that those who do such things will not inherit the kingdom of God.

The works of the flesh are the behaviors that characterize those living **without** God, those who remain unredeemed, unsaved – the normal, everyday people of the fallen world. And these works of the flesh just naturally flow out of the life that is ruled by the flesh. People don't have to learn to do the works of the flesh. You don't have to practice having jealousy or envy, it comes naturally. You don't need to be coached into being sensual and having impure thoughts. These things are already baked into the fallen human condition. They are already in there, and will find ways to be expressed.

The fruit of the Spirit would then represent the characteristic attitudes and behaviors of those who are living with God, who are being led by the Spirit and belong to Jesus Christ. This fruit of the Spirit represents something which would be important to eventually find in the lives of those claiming to be followers of Jesus Christ. So then, somehow, in some way, we have to get from being people whose lives actively express the works of the flesh, to being people whose lives demonstrate the fruit of the Spirit. But if you haven't noticed there is a problem in the church world.

DISCUSSION QUESTIONS:

1 – Can you think of any contemporary ways in which people attempt to gain justification apart from faith in Jesus Christ?

2 – How can walking in the Spirit create conflicts in our lives?

3 – Describe at least one way you understand that you need to deny yourself and take up your cross.

2 THE MATURITY PROBLEM

There is, among those who are churched people, a pretty wide-spread failure to mature spiritually. But this is not a new thing. The early church leaders noticed this trend and complained about it.

> *I Corinthians 3:1-4   But I, brothers, could not address you as spiritual people, but as people of the flesh, as infants in Christ. 2 I fed you with milk, not solid food, for you were not ready for it. And even now you are not yet ready, 3 for you are still of the flesh. For while there is jealousy and strife among you, are you not of the flesh and behaving only in a human way?*

The people of the Corinthian church had to be given milk rather than solid food, because they could not handle the solid stuff. As a result of their under-developed condition, they just couldn't digest the more meaty spiritual food. And what was the evidence of their immaturity? There was jealousy and strife among them. They were competitive with each other. They were jealous over each other's position or treatment within the congregation. This means they were not loving, patient, kind or good. They were striving against each other rather than striving for each other. They were looking out for their own interests instead of prioritizing the interests of others. They were squabbling and jockeying for position in a way that said fairly loudly and clearly, "me first." Jealousy, strife, and resentment, filled the church. They were offended by each other rather than celebrating each other's blessings and successes.

> *Hebrews 5:11-14   About this we have much to say, and it is hard to explain, since you have become dull of hearing. 12 For though by this time you ought to be teachers, you need someone to teach you again the basic principles of the oracles of God. You need milk, not solid food, 13 for everyone who lives on milk is unskilled in the word of righteousness, since he is a child. 14 But solid food is for the mature, for those who have their powers of discernment trained by constant practice to distinguish good from evil.*

The writer of Hebrews was saying very much

the same thing to the recipients of His letter that Paul was saying to the Corinthians. There was an expectation of a certain maturity that should have been reached by this time in their experience. But the people just weren't there yet. If the expected level of maturity had been attained, then the whole letter, the whole conversation, could have been completely different. But the failure to grow had made the people hard of hearing. It made them unskilled in the word of righteousness. And since they were unskilled in the word, they could not hear more mature things. Though they should have been teaching others at this point, instead they still needed the kind of nurturing care that newborn believers need. They still had to be told over and over again not to fight with each other, not to be jealous of each other and to stop fussing about childish things and to start adulting.

Have you heard of failure to launch syndrom? Psychologists describe it as a syndrome in which young adults have failed to mature into adulthood to the point that they can't function without their parents help. It's that thirty-year-old guy living in his parent's basement playing video games all day. Are we growing up spiritually? Are we maturing? Or are we failing to launch?

The different aspects of the Fruit of the Spirit, the nine different virtues, are the outward evidences and the practical results of the indwelling, sanctifying work of the Holy Spirit. They reflect His work of conforming us to the image and likeness of Jesus Christ. They are progressively developed in our lives as believers, and their presence in our lives can give us something of a measurement of our progress in sanctification. And, of course, it is good to have a way of measuring our progress. After all, the Lord has told us in II Corinthians 13:5, "examine yourselves to see if you are in the faith." Psalm 119:59 says, "I considered my ways and turned my feet to your testimonies." Lamentations 3:40 says, "Let us examine and probe our ways, and return to the Lord." So, the Lord wants us to keep tabs on our personal progress. He wants us to have a realistic view of how we are doing. And of course, one clear way to see if you are in the faith is to check and see how the progress of bearing the fruit of the Spirit is going on in you. How am I doing now with these virtues compared to how I was doing a few years ago? Am I loving my brothers and sisters in the Lord more than I used to? Am I more patient? Am I more faithful? Am I kinder than I used to be? Do I have more self-control than I did last year?

These are very relevant questions, because God's metrics for success are not the same as man's metrics for success. When we try to check up on our progress in obtaining the fruit of the Spirit, we don't compare ourselves to other people. And the reason for that is that we are all different. In any given congregation there will be some newer converts who are just beginning the process of being progressively sanctified, and there will be some grizzled old veterans of the faith with scars and fruit to prove it. And there will be many others in between at various stages of development. If you are a person who has travelled down a few roads in the Christian life and you compare yourself to those who don't have as much experience, then you could expose yourself to the dangers of pride. If you are a person of less experience and you compare yourself to more seasoned people of the faith, that might lead you to unnecessary self-condemnation. So, we do not compare ourselves to other people to test our progress. The only two comparisons that make any sense are the following.

(1) Comparing ourselves to the Lord Jesus Christ who is our standard. And, of course, none of us will ever measure up in that comparison. But He is the standard of all standards to follow and to chase after in imitation. So, it makes sense to compare ourselves to the Lord's perfection.

(2) Comparing ourselves today to ourselves at some time in the past. Which could lead us

to ask some questions. Have I improved in my actual attitudes and behaviors? Do I care more if my life is pleasing to the Lord? Do I have the joy of the Lord in me more now than in the past? Do I find myself being a more faithful person than I once was?

DISCUSSION QUESTIONS:

1 – What do you think can hinder the growth of Christians?

2 – Why is it unwise to compare yourself with others in the church?

3 – Can you find at least one area in your life where you have grown compared to where you were a couple of years ago?

3 THE TENSION

There is a kind of tension in the life of someone seeking to be fruitful. Some scripture passages urge us to be still and trust God. In many ways we are told not to act but to simply trust. We read that "He who began this work in you will complete it" (Philippians 1:6). If God began the work in me and it is He who will finish it, what am I to do? We also read that we are "predestined to be conformed to the image of Jesus" (Romans 8:29). If we are predestined to be conformed, can anything we do or don't do change the plan? These sorts of scripture passages tend to lead us to wait patiently for God to do what only God can do. While other passages urge us to exert effort in the process. We read that we are to "put off some things and to put on Christ" (Ephesians 4:22, I Peter 2:1, Romans 13:14). We read that we are to "cleanse ourselves of every defilement" (II Corinthians 7:1). We are told to "strive for peace and to strive for holiness" (Hebrews 12:14). Our spiritual lives require a balance between work and rest. A balance between resting in the fact that God has begun a work in us and knowing that it is He who will complete it – and putting forth the effort that He demands from us in the transformation process. We are simultaneously called upon to rest and to act.

This means that there are a couple of different ways that we could go wrong in our attempts to cultivate the fruit of the Spirit in our lives. We could take the pure "God is sovereign so don't worry about it" approach, also known as antinomianism. With this approach we are completely free from the law and have nothing to really obey, since the sovereignty of God will take care of everything. Or we could err on the other side and become overly legalistic and live like the Pharisees, demanding unrealistic things from ourselves and others. But a balance needs to be struck between the two.

The sincere willingness to work hard at obedience can often be good and right. The Bible frequently encourages us towards obedience, which is doing something active to work hard on our attitudes, to work on our humility, to strive to imitate Jesus Christ. We should approach our spiritual lives with this kind of intentionality because God clearly reveals to us important matters of obedience in His word. Jesus said "if you love me, do what I say" (John 14:15). But if our spiritual lives depended only on our hard work and just all out neglected faith in and dependence on God, we would end up spiritually exhausted and discouraged. Our work alone, even if it is diligent and sustained, can't achieve our spiritual transformation. We need to rest as well as work, believing prayerfully that God is at work in us, drawing us closer into the life that He desires for us to live.

What does a life look like that has both of these things? What is it like to have full trust and sincere reliance on God's work in our lives and also not be neglecting our own responsibility to act in sanctification? I think it is really not that hard to understand. For example, it's our responsibility to read the Word of God regularly. God isn't going to do that part for us. But as we read, we should be expressing and believing in God's help to our understanding. As we do our utmost to learn from God's word, we need to maintain our reliance on the Holy Spirit for opening the eyes of our understanding and for our ultimate transformation. We should pray as we study, asking the Lord to give us understanding in each passage of scripture we read. We should implore the God of all grace to bring about changes in our attitudes and desires. We should strive for, dream of, hope for and pray for our own transformation.

What could your life look like? What would life be like if the fruit of the Spirit was consistently being evidenced in your life? How different can you be from your old original sin shaped person? How much can you be transformed? How much like Jesus can you become? And what will be the impact of that transformation on the world around you? How will your changes affect the people who know you? What would it be like to be a truly loving person always kind to and very patient with others? What would it be like to be a person who always had the interests of others in mind, even above your own interests? What would it be like to be a person of real, consistent self-control and faithfulness? I'll tell you what it would be like, it would be amazing! It would be the most fulfilling, joyful impactful life possible for us to have.

God wants all of us to work with Him in the sanctification process. He wants us to cooperate with Him so that He can begin and continue the process of molding, shaping, and transforming us into the express image of His Son, Jesus Christ. He wants to make us into a better and more holy people. He wants to transform us by the renewing of our minds. He wants to remove our old way of thinking about things. He wants to put right thinking into our thought process.

It is by the power of the Holy Spirit that this sanctification process is done. However, you will not be a passive robot in all of this. And I am in no way denying the sovereignty of God when I say this. You cannot take the sovereignty of God away from me. I would die rather than give it up. That is how important it is to me. But you will not be a passive robot in the sanctification process. You have to be willing to work in cooperation with the Holy Spirit once He begins this work in you. Your job will be to get into the Word, to read the Bible, to listen intently to sermons, to pray, to participate in the fellowship of the saints - in order to find out exactly what it is that God wants to change about you. Your job will be to take advantage of all the means of grace while staying sensitive to what the Lord may be revealing to you. You will need to find out which ungodly qualities the Lord is bringing to your attention, so that you will **"put them off,"** and which godly qualities He will want you to **"put on."** Even though this is a work of the Holy Spirit in you, it cannot succeed without you trying. God produces the fruit but you won't become fruitful by not trying. While it is true that you cannot produce the fruit of the Spirit in your own life by simply trying to do so, it is equally true that you will never be someone who bears fruit without trying. The sovereignty of God is true, and the responsibility of man is true. Both are clearly delineated in the Bible. One being true doesn't make the other one untrue. As Jesus welcomes His followers into eternity, what does He say to them? He says "well done." As if they actually did something, right? He says to them "well done, good and faithful servants." And then, they say to Him, "When did we do anything? We didn't do anything. You, Lord, did it all!" And you know what? They are both right.

DISCUSSION QUESTIONS:

1 – Describe the tension between work and rest in the Christian growth process.

2 – If we are predestined to be conformed to the character and image of Jesus Christ, why do we need to act at all in the process?

3 – Describe a way in which you might need to take action in the sanctification process.

4 BEARING FRUIT REQUIRES PATIENCE

> Galatians 6:9   And let us not grow weary of doing good, for in due season we will reap, if we do not give up.

There is an "if we don't give up" clause in this harvest promise. In due season we will reap, if we do not give up. When is due season? After the seed has been sown and cultivated and watered for a while, the "due season" will arrive. However, seasons can seem long sometimes. You plant in the spring, but you don't harvest until the fall. It is in our own best interest to keep doing good, to continue sowing the right seed, until either something happens here on earth and some kind of a harvest comes our way, or we are taken home to receive the full harvest of our work there. The harvest that we are here being called upon to hope for is not some earthly, physical blessing. It is the harvest of bearing the fruit of the Spirit. If we keep doing good, it is inevitable that good will come of it.

> *Philippians 3:12-15 Not that I have already obtained this or am already perfect, but I press on to make it my own, because Christ Jesus has made me his own. 13 Brothers, I do not consider that I have made it my own. But one thing I do: forgetting what lies behind and straining forward to what lies ahead, 14 I press on toward the goal for the prize of the upward call of God in Christ Jesus. 15 Let those of us who are mature think this way, and if in anything you think otherwise, God will reveal that also to you.*

The apostle Paul taught that it takes a lifetime to attain what sometimes feels like an elusive goal of knowing Jesus Christ and being conformed to His character. Even with all of his extraordinary missionary accomplishments and spiritual effort, Paul concluded that he still had not reached his goal. Writing this letter to the Philippians, Paul wasn't thinking of the spiritual ground that he had already covered. He wasn't exulting in his successes or self-reproaching about his failures. Instead, he was resolute about keeping his focus and pressing ahead. Then he says this amazing thing, "All of us, then, who are mature should think this way." Think which way? The way that knows you aren't there yet and you have to keep fighting until your days are over. All of us who are mature ought to think like this. We ought to be people who press forward and strain ahead, always advancing toward the prize. Those who think they have the Christian life mastered may actually have made the least progress. But those who begin to understand the gap between themselves and a holy, God may be the most advanced in godliness.

Spiritual growth is hard to measure. Progress and failure may be difficult to quantify. Humility, however, may be the sure sign that seeds of transformation have been planted and are being nourished. Humility is key for pressing ahead in the Christian life. "Success," or progress in our obedience, cannot be credited to our own efforts, and of course progress is no reason for a smug attitude and no reason for complacency. Neither is "failure" a way we disqualify ourselves from grace. In fact, failure may end up being the best teacher. I can tell you by very personal experience that failure is a powerful teacher. The second time you face a situation or a temptation you probably do better than the first time. The initial failure can fix our resolve to face the second go around with more determination. We can faithfully "forget" our past sins and advance with confidence in Christ.

It does takes time to grow fruit, and it requires care and cultivation to get good fruit. When the Lord talks about fruitfulness, He often uses farming analogies. The sower sows the seed. He scatters it out to all the hearers. For some people, the seed falls into good soil and grows. In others, it starts to grow, but then stops. In still others it produces a finished crop; some more, some less. But by using the farming analogy I think the Lord is letting us know that the good fruit may take a little time to develop and become visible and useful.

You know the truth; whatever you sow, that is what you will reap. Well, maybe you have been sowing bad seed in some particular area of your life for so long that it will take a bit of time for the good seed you are sowing now to produce a good crop. Like the guy who repents in prison; he is forgiven now, he is spiritually free, but he still has to reap what he previously sowed until the next time of harvest comes around. He still has to finish his sentence. Like the character in the movie, "O Brother, Where Art Thou?" He got saved and baptized while being an escapee from prison, so he thought that the forgiveness of God meant he wouldn't have to go back to prison. If a person has been selfish all their life, and now they have come to faith in Jesus, will they be completely unselfish by tomorrow? Probably not. But it will come if they don't quit. He who began a good work in you will see it through to completion.

DISCUSSION QUESTIONS:

1 – Why is patience required in the one who desires to bear the fruit of the Spirit?

2 – Do you find yourself striving with more effort for earthly things or for godly character?

3 – In what ways can you "press on" to make the upward call of God in Christ Jesus your goal?

5 WHY SHOULD WE
BEAR FRUIT?

(1) TO GLORIFY GOD

> *John 15:8   By this my Father is glorified, that you bear much fruit and so prove to be my disciples.*

Bearing fruit glorifies God. Bearing fruit causes the glory of God to be seen by others. To bring glory to God is one of our main functions as believers. And, of course, the desire to bring glory to God infuses every heart that truly knows and loves the Lord. If you know Him, your deepest desire is going to be to make Him known in such a way that people are drawn to Him. If you love Him, your big dream will be to see other people come to know how glorious, how amazing, how wonderful, and how perfect He is. The grateful heart whose eyes have been opened to His glory desires nothing more than to bring that glory to light in every way possible. If the urge to make the greatness and goodness of God known to others is not in you, then maybe you should question where you are in the faith. Indifference is an unhealthy response to our call to make the Lord known.

To declare God with your voice, and yet show by your life no evidence of the fruit that comes from being with Him - this does the opposite of bringing glory to God. First then, we ought to bear fruit to bring the glory to God that He deserves. When people see an obvious contradiction between what is spoken and what is lived out, it has a deflating impact and carries the aroma of hypocracy.

(2) TO PROVE BY DEMONSTRATION THAT WE ARE DISCIPLES OF THE LORD

John 15:8   By this my Father is glorified, that you bear much fruit and so prove to be my disciples.

Matthew 7:16-17   You will recognize them by their fruits. Are grapes gathered from thornbushes, or figs from thistles? 17 So, every healthy tree bears good fruit, but the diseased tree bears bad fruit

Bearing fruit is the one clear way to demonstrate that you are the Lord's true disciple. Without such fruit being developed in you, in fact, the exact opposite is being demonstrated for the world to see. You can't grow figs on a thornbush. So, if thorns are the visible fruit of your life, then, clearly, you are an unhealthy tree. Fruit nourishes. Thorns stab. So then, your life cannot be something that just constantly stabs other people and be a good, true testimony. Your life ought to nourish others and feed others rather than harm others. A true disciple's life is a life that nourishes others with the fruits of the Spirit. A tree does not eat its own fruit. The fruit of our lives is not for us. It is by nature for others, and is meant to nourish and serve others.

John 13:35   By this all people will know that you are my disciples, if you have love for one another."

The Lord Himself told us that the love we have for one another will be the evidence to the people of the world that we are indeed His true disciples. Without this fruit of the Spirit which is love, we will look just like anybody else living on the earth. Nothing will make us stand out. Nothing about our lives will indicate that we sincerely belong to Jesus Christ. So, to bear fruit then is necessary in order for us to prove that we are genuine, true, real-life disciples of our great Lord.

(3) WE ARE APPOINTED TO BEAR FRUIT

> *John 15:16   You did not choose me, but I chose you and appointed you that you should go and bear fruit and that your fruit should abide, so that whatever you ask the Father in my name, he may give it to you.*

Bearing fruit is what we are supposed to do as Christians. Bearing fruit is the destiny of everyone who is chosen to be a disciple of Jesus Christ. We have been called to bear fruit, and if we are the real deal, we certainly will. Bearing fruit is part of our call. Bearing fruit is so natural to the true disciple that he cannot not bear fruit.

If you are somewhat anxious over the lack of fruit in your life, then here is what you do: make yourself available to all the means of grace, all the ways that grace gets into you and does what it does. Read your Bible, pray, be present at every opportunity to hear the preaching and teaching of the word, get involved in active fellowship - and you will begin to see changes take place in the fruitfulness of your life. These things are known as the normal means of grace; Bible study, prayer, fellowship, etc.

DISCUSSION QUESTIONS:

1 – How does bearing the fruit of the Spirit glorify God?

2 – In what way does bearing the fruit of the Spirit prove one's discipleship?

3 – If a Christian does not avail themselves of the normal means of grace, what will likely happen to their spiritual life?

6 WHAT IS BEARING FRUIT?

(1) LIVING A RIGHTEOUS LIFE – HAVING GOOD WORKS

> *Philippians 1:9-11   And it is my prayer that your love may abound more and more, with knowledge and all discernment, 10 so that you may approve what is excellent, and so be pure and blameless for the day of Christ, 11 filled with the fruit of righteousness that comes through Jesus Christ, to the glory and praise of God.*

Paul's prayer for the Philippians is that they would love more. And he prays that day after day their ability to be fruitful with the fruit of love would increase as time goes on. And he prays that the quality of their love would improve through gaining more knowledge and discernment. And he prays that their lives would overflow with the fruit of righteousness that comes through Jesus Christ.

> Colossians 1:10   so as to walk in a manner worthy of the Lord, fully pleasing to him: bearing fruit in every good work and increasing in the knowledge of God;

Those who bear fruit can be seen as being more righteous in their living than they once were. There needs to be evidence in our lives that the teaching we are hearing is having an impact. There needs to be evident works in our lives that weren't there before.

Bearing fruit is us living lives that are worthy of the Lord. It is us living lives that are more and more fully pleasing to Him. And the evidence, or proof, of living such lives that are more pleasing to the Lord is what we do, the works we do. This means living lives with more and more love in our interactions with people. It means actively demonstrating more patience, kindness and goodness toward others. It means living with more peace in our hearts, more faithfulness and greater self-control.

(2) GROWING IN GRACE

> II Peter 3:18   *But grow in the grace and knowledge of our Lord and Savior Jesus Christ. To*

*him be the glory both now and to the day
of eternity. Amen.*

The grace we have been given is meant
to produce Christ-like attitudes and behaviors in
us. As we receive the grace of God through His
appointed means of grace, we become different
than we once were. We become more gracious
ourselves towards others. We learn that, rather
than exposing the faults of others, love covers a
multitude of sins. We learn that those who have
been forgiven so much, must also be great forgivers
of others. The Bible tells us that Jesus was full of
grace (John 1:14). As imitators of Him, this is who
we gradually must become also. We must be people
who grow in grace.

(3) GROWING IN THE KNOWLEDGE OF GOD

*Colossians 1:10   so as to walk in a manner
worthy of the Lord, fully pleasing to him: bearing
fruit in every good work and increasing in the
knowledge of God;*

*II Peter 3:18   But grow in the grace and
knowledge of our Lord and Savior Jesus Christ. To
him be the glory both now and to the day
of eternity. Amen.*

Jesus, in John 1:14, is full of grace and truth. His truth must also become a priority in our discipleship. As we grow in the knowledge of our God, we are more enabled to grow into imitators of Him. Without proper training in doctrine and truth, we cannot possibly be transformed. For that reason, it is vital for the believer to become an active student of the Bible. So, growing in the knowledge of God is an important part of bearing fruit.

(4) EXHIBITING THE FRUIT OF THE SPIRIT IN OUR LIVES

> *Galatians 5:22-23   But the fruit of the Spirit is love, joy, peace, patience, kindness, goodness, faithfulness, 23 gentleness, self-control; against such things there is no law.*

These nine aspects of the fruit of the Spirit are given to us as particular character traits which our lives ought to express. This provides us with clear goals to aim for. We don't have to wonder what we ought to be like. We know that we ought to be loving, joyful, peaceful, patient, kind, good, faithful, gentle people with self-control. Growth in these virtues is what we want to see in ourselves. Over time we want to see, not that we are kinder than so and so, not that we are more faithful than someone else, but that these things have increased in us individually. We want to see that we are kinder, gentler, more patient than we used to be.

DISCUSSION QUESTIONS:

1 – Which aspects of the fruit of the Spirit can you see in the others of your group?

2 – How does growing in the knowledge of God help you to grow spiritually?

3 – Which of the nine aspects of the fruit of the Spirit would you most like to grow in?

7 WHAT CAUSES US TO BEAR FRUIT?

(1) PRAYER

Jeremiah 33:3   Call to me and I will answer you, and will tell you great and hidden things that you have not known.

Many would say that prayer is asking God for the things we need. But in Jeremiah 33:3, prayer is also connected to revelation. It is an invitation to pray and to learn new things. It was in prayer where Solomon was granted the wisdom to lead his people. It was in his time wrestling with God in prayer where Jacob was transformed and became Israel. It was in the desperate pleas of Hannah where Samson was conceived. It is often in those moments alone with the Lord where destinies are set in stone, where new things are birthed, and where true transformation begins.

> *Matthew 7:7-8   Ask, and it will be given to you; seek, and you will find; knock, and it will be opened to you. 8 For everyone who asks receives, and the one who seeks finds, and to the one who knocks it will be opened.*

Ask, seek, knock – the ones who ask receive, the ones who seek find, the ones who knock get the opened door.   We know that pride comes before a fall and that humility comes before growth into reward and elevation.   Humility is needed then for spiritual growth.   Pride says, "I've got this." Humility says "help me, I need your help, Lord." So then, the humility of prayer is involved in fruitfulness.   Prayer, when it is sincere, is an act of humility. We rarely go to the Lord in our pride, because we feel like we have things under control.   But when we have run out of personal options, when we are feeling desperation, then we go humbly to the only One who can change us.

(2) FELLOWSHIP

> *I Corinthians 14:26   What then, brothers? When you come together, each one has a hymn, a lesson, a revelation, a tongue, or an interpretation. Let all things be done for building up.*

Our being together, our gathering in fellowship is meant to have the impact of building us up in the faith, of causing each other to grow. In our mutual love for the Lord, we are enabled to stir each other up to do the right thing and to do good things.

> *Hebrews 10:24-25   And let us consider how to stir up one another to love and good works, 25 not neglecting to meet together, as is the habit of some, but encouraging one another, and all the more as you see the day drawing near.*

As we spend time in each other's company, we gain a deeper understanding of each other's sufferings, victories, proclivities, and more. This stirs us up in love toward one another. This serves as a mutual call to action, so that we are all stirred up or provoked into the action of doing good works. In the Christian atmosphere of fellowship, there is freedom. Freedom to confess our sins. Freedom to be held accountable for our behaviors.

(3) ABIDING

> *John 15:4-5   Abide in me, and I in you. As the branch cannot bear fruit by itself, unless it abides in the vine, neither can you, unless you*

abide in me. 5 I am the vine; you are the branches. Whoever abides in me and I in him, he it is that bears much fruit, for apart from me you can do nothing

We are commanded to abide in the Lord's word (John 8:31,) and to abide in His love (John 15:10). In very real ways, we are completely incapable of pulling this off on our own. We need Him to help us to abide in Him. It is God Himself who causes us to abide in Him, to remain in Him. But there is a part for us to play. The spiritual disciplines of prayer and Bible study, and fellowship will go a long way towards maximizing what God does in us. To abide in His word is to relish it and crave it for all the powerful things His word can do in us. It has the power to reach down into the deepest part of a person and make a fundamental change. To abide in His love is to love as He loves; to give more grace to others, to be more merciful, to be quick to forgive, and to seek the good of our brothers and sisters in the Lord.

(4) PRUNING

John 15:2 Every branch in me that does not bear fruit he takes away, and every branch that does bear fruit he prunes, that it may bear more fruit.

The Lord has solution for us when our fruitfulness is too low. When we are not quite producing the kind of fruit we ought to be producing, God has a remedy. He calls His solution to this, "pruning." This is actually a great promise from the Lord. If we are struggling with the amount of fruit we are producing, He promises to intervene in our lives through pruning in order to increase our fruitfulness. What is pruning? It is cutting away unhealthy unproductive parts of a plant, so that the nutrients will be more focused on the productive parts. This might involve some discomfort which the Lord brings to us with the purpose of helping us to realize that whatever we are doing is not spiritually productive. It could involve some painful moment which has the effect of turning you around or refocusing you. We may sometimes find ourselves asking "Why, Lord? Why am I suffering like this? What is going on here?" Maybe He is pruning us in order to make us more fruitful, so that He can later reward us for our fruitfulness which He alone caused. I would include in the concept of pruning in almost any discipline from the Lord to our lives.

> *Hebrews 12:11   For the moment all discipline seems painful rather than pleasant, but later it yields the peaceful fruit of righteousness to those who have been trained by it.*

(5) TRUSTING IN THE LORD

> *Jeremiah 17:7-8*   *"Blessed is the man who trusts in the Lord, whose trust is the Lord. 8 He is like a tree planted by water, that sends out its roots by the stream, and does not fear when heat comes, for its leaves remain green, and is not anxious in the year of drought, for it does not cease to bear fruit."*

In life, there is so much that is really out of our hands. There are so many things that we cannot control, that it can feel like chaos has taken over and everything is spinning so fast that we can't seem to be able to get a grip on things. For such things and for such times – we trust the Lord. This trust puts us in a position of being near to the thing we need, in order to stay healthy and fruitful. The one who trusts is like a tree that is planted right by the water. The one who trusts the Lord can even be fruitful in a time of drought. Our condition does not depend on our immediate environment in the world, if we are trusting in the Lord, because we remain near to the refreshing waters of the Lord's provision. We can remain green and fruitful no matter what.

(6) BEING TAUGHT

Ephesians 4:11-13   And he gave the apostles, the prophets, the evangelists, the shepherds and teachers, 12 to equip the saints for the work of ministry, for building up the body of Christ, 13 until we all attain to the unity of the faith and of the knowledge of the Son of God, to mature manhood, to the measure of the stature of the fullness of Christ,

Being taught the word of God enables us to bear fruit. God has faithfully provided us with the foundation of the church's teaching through the early Apostles. The original Apostles were given the great gift and calling of writing the New Testament for us. Their lives and their work represent gifts, or presents, given on our behalf so that we know the truths of God that we need in order to become and remain healthy. And in addition to that, the Lord has also given us men in our own time to be pastors and teachers who can present the word of God to us in an understandable and profitable way. Our spiritual growth is facilitated and accelerated through their giftings. But, of course, we are required to remain teachable. You probably have an understanding of what it means to be teachable. It means that you give up your right to be offended by correction. It means that when you hear what the Lord is saying to you, you come to agree with Him no matter what your first reaction was. It means you don't let pride steal your chance to grow.

Proverbs 12:1   Whoever loves discipline loves knowledge, but he who hates reproof is stupid.

Proverbs 29:1   He who is often reproved, yet stiffens his neck, will suddenly be broken beyond healing.

A person could throw away their own chance to grow by letting the sensitivity of pride overcome the humility of learning. Maybe you are sitting in church, hearing a sermon, and in that sermon, something hits you. It hits you hard because it is a truth that exposes something wrong in you to you. That moment when conviction happens is important. It is good, it is valuable, it is a growth moment. But sometimes it is a hard to hear moment. How you respond at that moment will be significant.

Mark 7:25-30   But immediately a woman whose little daughter had an unclean spirit heard of him and came and fell down at his feet. 26 Now the woman was a Gentile, a Syrophoenician by birth. And she begged him to cast the demon out of her daughter. 27 And he said to her, "Let the children be fed first, for it is not right to take the children's bread and throw it to the dogs." 28 But she answered him, "Yes, Lord; yet even the dogs under the table eat the children's crumbs." 29 And he said to her, "For this statement you may go your way; the demon has left your daughter." 30 And she went home and found the child lying in bed and the demon gone.

Those who have been corrected by God know that it truly is the truth that sets one free. The truth is sharp and gets right to the point. It may pierce deep down into us to reveal things we would rather keep hidden, even from ourselves, but who can deny that it does its work thoroughly and powerfully. The Syrophoenician woman above came to the Lord for help. He helped her by doing what she asked of Him. But He truly helped her in an even more significant and eternal way. He made her one of His own people that day. If the Lord revels your true nature to you, do as this woman did. If the Lord calls you a dog, agree with Him, because He is always right. Say, "Yes, Lord, I am a dog as you say. But please help me anyway!"

(7) DELIGHTING IN THE WORD OF GOD

Psalm 1:1-3   Blessed is the man who walks not in the counsel of the wicked, nor stands in the way of sinners, nor sits in the seat of scoffers; 2 but his delight is in the law of the Lord, and on his

> *law he meditates day and night. 3 He is like a tree*
> *planted by streams of water that yields its fruit in*
> *its season, and its leaf does not wither. In all that*
> *he does, he prospers.*

Blessed is the one whose delight is in the law, or the word, of the Lord. Being people who delight in the law of the Lord, in this passage, means those who love His word and spend time in it. Delighting in His word and avoiding the counsels of the wicked and the sinners and the scoffers, enables us to grow stronger in the Lord. To delight in the word of God is a step beyond being dedicated to reading it on a regular basis. To delight in the word is to want it as a governing priority in your life. It is to hunger and thirst for righteousness. It is to crave what the word of God can do in us. It is to be filled, or satisfied from what the word alone can provide for us.

DISCUSSION QUESTIONS:

1 – How does fellowship help you grow spiritually?

2 – How does listening to preaching help you grow spiritually?

3 – Are you a generally teachable person? Are you able to humbly receive correction?

8 THE CONSEQUENCES OF UNFRUITFULNESS

The consequences of living an unfruitful life are so tragic and so terrifying for the unbeliever, that all who hear of them should tremble and strive with everything they have to avoid such a fate. Unbelievers are by nature completely unfruitful. Being spiritually dead, they cannot grow in grace or knowledge. And if they should remain in this condition, their fate is terrifying.

> *Matthew 7:19   Every tree that does not bear good fruit is cut down and thrown into the fire.*

The God of all creation has an expectation of timely fruitfulness for all that He has made. He has created all living things with the purpose that they multiply and yield fruit. The Lord, in His teachable monent encounter with an unproductive fig tree, brings that truth home powerfully.

> *Matthew 21:18-19   In the morning, as he was returning to the city, he became hungry. 19 And seeing a fig tree by the wayside, he went to it and found nothing on it but only leaves. And he said to it, "May no fruit ever come from you again!" And the fig tree withered at once.*

At the time when the Lord expects to find fruit, it better be there. Opportunity is not forever. This particular fig tree had experienced its last chance to prove itself as a producer of figs. The consequences were dire and ultimate. The entire nation of Judah found itself facing similar straits with their long history of unfruitfulness, when God spoke to them through the prophet Isaiah.

> *Isaiah 5:1-7   Let me sing for my beloved my love song concerning his vineyard: My beloved had a vineyard on a very fertile hill. 2 He dug it and cleared it of stones, and planted it with choice vines; he built a watchtower in the midst of it, and hewed out a wine vat in it; and he looked for it to yield grapes, but it yielded wild grapes. 3 And now, O inhabitants of Jerusalem and men of Judah, judge between me and my vineyard. 4 What more was there to do for my vineyard, that I have not done in it? When I looked for it to yield grapes, why did it yield wild grapes? 5 And now I will tell you what I will do to my vineyard.*

I will remove its hedge, and it shall be devoured; I will break down its wall, and it shall be trampled down. 6 I will make it a waste; it shall not be pruned or hoed, and briers and thorns shall grow up; I will also command the clouds that they rain no rain upon it. 7 For the vineyard of the Lord of hosts is the house of Israel, and the men of Judah are his pleasant planting; and he looked for justice, but behold, bloodshed; for righteousness, but behold, an outcry!

When the Lord looks for justice, love, righteousness, joy, peace, patience and all the fruits He loves to see in the lives of His people, may He find what He is looking for. When He looks for fruit in our lives, may He find it in abundance! But there comes a time in every life when the decisions that have been made are considered to be final. Remember how Esau gave no significant value to his birthright, but easily and nonchalantly sold it for a single bowl of soup to his brother Jacob? Later in life, Esau sought repentance with tears, but could not find it (Hebrews 12:17). He sought for, but could not find or muster up within himself any sense of repentance. The fact that he sought repentance with tears indicates that he regretted his decision. But the only regret he had was likely a regret for the consequences, and not a regret for the attitude of not valuing what God had given him. He did not care for the punishment, which was a kind of spiritual emptiness and a sense of lost opportunity. But he only regretted the consequence.

Among believers, we know that there is the possibility of being less fruitful than one ought to be. The consequences of a less fruitful life being lived by a believer are seen in a number of scriptures. We saw some examples of these scriptures in chapter two. And here we will look some others.

> *Luke 13:6-9   And he told this parable: "A man had a fig tree planted in his vineyard, and he came seeking fruit on it and found none. 7 And he said to the vinedresser, 'Look, for three years now I have come seeking fruit on this fig tree, and I find none. Cut it down. Why should it use up the ground?' 8 And he answered him, 'Sir, let it alone this year also, until I dig around it and put on manure. 9 Then if it should bear fruit next year, well and good; but if not, you can cut it down.'"*

Here we see that effort from the Lord has been put into cultivating this fig tree. Much has been done in order to make it productive and fruitful, but nothing has worked so far. The attempts to make it fruitful have continued for three years already. This shows God's great patience and longsuffering as He works to make us fruitful. One more year is then given to the effort. Time for change is not unlimited.

One of the consequences of delayed fruit bearing in your life may be the need to pile manure all around your life to finally get something sparked through extra fertilization. God, the great cultivator, the vine dresser, will do whatever it takes to get some fruit out of your life. Being a good and true Father, He will discipline His children in order to bring about the character changes that He desires in them. If all of the ordinary means of grace are failing to produce fruit in your life, then He will take extraordinary steps to ensure your eventual productivity.

Hebrews 12:11   For the moment all discipline seems painful rather than pleasant, but later it yields the peaceful fruit of righteousness to those who have been trained by it.

The consequences of delayed fruit bearing may be the discipline of the Lord. A spiritual spanking may be in store for you if the fruits you were designed to bear are not ripening properly. Our response to the discipline of God is very important to our level of fruitfulness. They are directly related. If you fail to receive the discipline of God with humility and repentance, then you are stuck where you are in your growth process. In fact, you will probably slip backwards and regress.

> *Proverbs 6:23   For the commandment is a lamp and the teaching a light, and the reproofs of discipline are the way of life,*

The reproofs of discipline are the way of life. This is to say that the end result of God's discipline to us is more life, more fruitfulness. Which helps us to see that the proper response to reproof, to discipline, to correction, is humble agreement with God. It may sometimes hurt our pride to be reproved. Correction can make us recoil at first. But in the end, the way of life is through the correction, through the reproof. So, my friends, it really, seriously and vitally helps us to be people who can be told we are doing it wrong without taking it personally and feeling insulted. God does not correct us just to be mean to us. He corrects us out of love so that we will be more conformed to the image of Jesus Christ. He corrects us to save us from remaining our old, stubborn, foolish selves.

> *Proverbs 10:17   Whoever heeds instruction is on the path to life, but he who rejects reproof leads others astray.*

The fruit that is produced in our lives will serve as at least part of the basis for individual rewards in the resurrection. In the parable of the minas, there are two men who receive heavenly rewards from the Lord (Luke 19:12-19). The size of their rewards directly corresponds with the degrees of fruitfulness they reached in their assigned responsibilities. They were rewarded according to what they did with the opportunities they were given. And so it will be for us. During the sanctification process, we become more transformed, more holy, more fruitful. And all that we have done in cooperation with the work of God in our brief time on the earth will play a role in what our ultimate state of reward will be. The Bible tells us that our work will be tested and the results will be a determining factor in our rewards (I Corinthians 3:10-15).

DISCUSSION QUESTIONS:

1 – What are the consequences of unfruitfulness for the unbeliever? What about for the believer?

2 – What is your biggest obstacle to receiving reproof and correction?

3 – Why is the way in which we receive reproof or correction so significant?

9 HOW THE WORLD DEFINES THE WORD LOVE

Galatians 5:22-23   But the fruit of the Spirit is love, joy, peace, patience, kindness, goodness, faithfulness, 23 gentleness, self-control; against such things there is no law.

Love is very likely the most misunderstood and wrongly defined word in the English language today. And although some of the world's ways of understanding love may come close to the truth, they are just misleading enough to send us down the wrong road of thinking about love. How is love described and understood in the world at large?

1 – LOVE IS PURELY EMOTION

Love is an intense feeling of deep affection.

Love is what one feels. It is like an emotional high, like a crush. It is a kind of emotional treat, and as long as an emotional treat is to be had, then love is believed to remain. But this kind of love hangs on a very weak thread. Like in a romantic scenario, love exists as long as there are excited feelings of infatuation. But experts tell us that the initial feeling of infatuation in a dating relationship only lasts from 1.5 to 3 years, and after that, something else better be there to hold everything together, because a simple crush cannot do it alone.

2 – LOVE IS PROVED BY BRINGING HAPPINESS

Or some could say that love is the responsibility of one person to make another person happy and to keep them happy. As long as you are making me happy, then I will love you. Or, as long as you are making me happy, then that proves that you love me. But the moment you stop pleasing me you are out because that proves you really don't love me. This love makes others responsible for my happiness. And gives them the impossible task of never unhappying me, or they will suffer the consequences of losing my love for them. This is a very self-centered love. It is even a kind of aggressive or violent love, because it threatens to be ungentle and unloving toward those who fail it.

3 – LOVE IS CONFIRMED BY AFFIRMATION

Or another way that someone may describe love today is to say that love is an affirmation of someone. Love is the approval and legitimization of a person's chosen behavior or lifestyle. This Kind of love is very popular today. It is the mainstream love. It is the Woke love. This kind of love never sees fault in the loved one, no matter what they do or believe. It is not allowed to even recognize evil in the loved one. This love forbids you from having any kind of moral code. This love will not permit the possibility of looking at any behavior in a negative way. This kind of love forbids judgement of any kind. It really even forbids discernment. This sort of love outlaws the whole concept of right and wrong. This affirming love removes any possibility of there being such a thing as tough love. Tough love is forbidden because it is making a judgement of what is best for you from outside of you. And certainly, tough love is not usually affirming.

These are some of the ways you might find the word love used in our culture today, and certainly these descriptions of love miss the mark.

DISCUSSION QUESTIONS:

1 – How is love more than simply a warm emotion toward others?

2 – Have you ever been guilty of pressuring others to prove their love to you by demanding a certain behavior or attitude?

3 – Why is it more loving to refuse to affirm the sinful lifestyle of a friend or family member?

10 LOVE IS OF GOD

So then, what is love? How should we define or describe it? The Bible tells us that God is love and has demonstrated that love in everything that he does. So, one way to understand love is to say that love is made clear and is pictured in the actions of the God, who is love. Paul compares faith, hope, and love, and concludes that "the greatest of these is love" (I Corinthians 13:12). Tim Keller defines love as serving a person for their good and intrinsic value, not for what the person brings to you. We know from the Lord that love is often sacrificial. "Greater love has no one than this, that someone lay down his life for his friend," (John 15:13). The Bible gives us a description of what love is like in...

> *I Corinthians 13:4-7   Love is patient and kind; love does not envy or boast; it is not arrogant 5 or rude. It does not insist on its own way; it is not irritable or resentful; 6 it does not rejoice at wrongdoing, but rejoices with the truth. 7 Love bears all things, believes all things, hopes all*

things, endures all things.

1 LOVE IS THE NATURE OF GOD

I John 4:8   Anyone who does not love does not know God, because God is love.

God is love.   God does not merely love; he is love. Everything that God does flows from his love. The gospel of John repeatedly informs us of the love of God the Father for God the Son, and of the love of God the Son for God the Father.

John 5:20   For the Father loves the Son and shows him all that he himself is doing. And greater works than these will he show him, so that you may marvel

John 17:22-23   The glory that you have given me I have given to them, that they may be one even as we are one, 23 I in them and you in me, that they may become perfectly one, so that the world may know that you sent me and loved them even as you loved me.

John 14:31a   but I do as the Father has commanded me, so that the world may know that

I love the Father.

Because the Father loves the Son, He made his will known to Him. Jesus in turn demonstrated his love to the Father through his submission and obedience. The theme of the entire Bible is the revelation of the God of love.

In the garden of Eden, God commanded that "you must not eat from the tree of the knowledge of good and evil, for when you eat of it you will surely die," (Genesis 2:17). To eat of this forbidden fruit, then, is a pretty serious thing. It is a dramatic and meaningful breaking of the covenant relationship between God and man. It is the kind of breach that would more than likely end a human relationship. It is like saying, "I'd rather die than be with you." It is a huge and shocking surprise then, when after Adam sins, God comes looking for him calling out, "Adam, Adam, where are you?" God seeks Adam, not to put him to death, but to reestablish a relationship with him. God is not coming for revenge or purely to punish Adam, but He is coming to correct and to restore. Adam's sin has broken the fellowship between him and God, but God's judgement is immediately mixed with mercy and the promise of even greater mercy to come. God, the One who is Love, will not allow sin to stand between him and the man whom He made in His own image. He personally steps into the problem to bring a merciful resolution. He seeks out Adam to create a bridge over the gap between them which Adam has made. That seeking and bridging continues throughout the Bible, and it reaches its loving pinnacle when God sends his Son into the world to rescue sinners and to provide them with eternal life on the cross. Jesus Christ, God the son, laying down His own life on our behalf is the most dramatic, poetic act of love the world has ever known. It is the defining moment of love in all of history for human beings.

I John 3:16   By this we know love, that he laid down his life for us, and we ought to lay down our lives for the brothers.

John declares, "This is how we know what love is: Jesus Christ laid down his life for us." And for this reason, we ought to lay down our lives for our brothers. So then, love has a large sacrificial element to it. We are offered an opportunity to enter into this love of God. But we are not just to sit back and receive. No, we are to stand up and participate by laying down our lives for others. And we know that God's love is not based on the merit of the recipient, so neither can our love be based on whether the loved ones deserve it.

Romans 5:7-8   For one will scarcely die for

ANDYRIPLEY

> *a righteous person—though perhaps for a good person one would dare even to die— 8 but God shows his love for us in that while we were still sinners, Christ died for us.*

So, of course, if our love for others is to be like God's love, then it should not be based on the merits of the recipients of our love. You mean I have to love my husband - I have to love my wife - no matter what they are like? Even if they aren't loving me back in the way that I want them to? Yes, that is what it means. That is how we imitate Jesus Christ. That is how we can be Christ-like, by loving others whether they love us back or not. The love that God loves with will sacrifice itself for the good of the loved ones. And God does not demand that His love be "earned" by some action on the part of the loved ones. This is beyond human love. It is other-worldly, foreign, purer, and more beautiful than any love found between fallen human beings.

2 GOD ALONE IS THE SOURCE OF LOVE

> *I John 4:19   We love because he first loved us.*

"Love the Lord Your God," we are commanded. We are totally incapable of loving either God or others - a condition that must be corrected by God before we can love. We are only made capable of loving after He first loves us (I John 4:19). So then, we must first become practical recipients of His love before we can turn around and love others in a true way. The Bible describes the process of making us capable of loving in different ways.

Circumcision of the heart...

> *Deuteronomy 30:6   And the Lord your God will circumcise your heart and the heart of your offspring, so that you will love the Lord your God with all your heart and with all your soul, that you may live.*

The old covenant was confirmed on man's side by the physical circumcision of men. This was an act done by men to men as a sign of agreement with the covenant made between God and man. But this new circumcision was to be different. It is not an operation performed by men. It is a spiritual surgery which can only be done by God Himself. It is a miraculous procedure preformed by the hand of God on a human heart which makes it capable of returning God's love. This was never possible in the fallen condition of man. This circumcision of the heart is the renewing of the man, it is the rebirth, it is the process of becoming "born again." It is the act whereby God takes the spirit of a human being and raises it from the dead. Since the fall of Adam, every human being is born spiritually dead. And as dead people, we are completely incapable of acting in any way. A dead person cannot move, cannot dream and cannot even hope for something. But by the hand of God, some unknown, deep surgery brings about the rebirth and re-enlivening of the spirit of a man. It is only this miracle of rebirth that makes any human being capable of loving God and of loving as God loves.

God's "writing his laws" on our hearts...

> *Jeremiah 31:33   For this is the covenant that I will make with the house of Israel after those days, declares the Lord: I will put my law within them, and I will write it on their hearts. And I will be their God, and they shall be my people.*

Jesus said to His disciples something to the effect of, "if you love Me, do what I say" (John 14:15). The idea being that those who love the Lord, who love their God, are people who obey Him. Love from the creature to the creator is evidenced by obedience. But we know that disobedience brought about the fall of man, and we know that ever since the fall, obedience has been basically impossible for man to accomplish. Which means that since the fall, it has been impossible for man to

– at least to some degree beyond what was formerly possible. This is wonderful news! With His law written on our hearts we are enabled to love His word, and to apply it with some success.

God removing our heart of stone and giving us a heart of flesh...

> *Ezekiel 11:19-20   And I will give them one heart, and a new spirit I will put within them. I will remove the heart of stone from their flesh and give them a heart of flesh, 20 that they may walk in my statutes and keep my rules and obey them. And they shall be my people, and I will be their God.*

That old heart of stone could not even desire to obey. It was cold and uncaring. It was unloving and entirely unresponsive to God and to His word. But now, the reborn man or woman can feel the desire to obey. They can know what it feels like to desire to please the Lord and be joyfully with Him. What a miracle that takes place and brings a new sensitivity to God and to what he wants from us. We turn from servants commanded to obey into children who delight to obey. There is a new sense of family. There is a new and powerful desire to be pleasing to our Father.

Removing old things and putting on new things...

Colossians 3:12-14   Put on then, as God's chosen ones, holy and beloved, compassionate hearts, kindness, humility, meekness, and patience, 13 bearing with one another and, if one has a complaint against another, forgiving each other; as the Lord has forgiven you, so you also must forgive. 14 And above all these, put on love, which binds everything together in perfect harmony.

The command to us then is to begin acting in the ways that we are commanded to act. We are to start loving and having the compassion we have been made capable of having. The very capacity to love is evidence of being born of God. We can now do what we could never before do. We can put up with each other. We can bear each other's weird eccentricities and foibles. We can endure, we can forgive and we can truly love. Once we are born again, all we have to do is act in these ways to be who we are meant to be.

I John 4:7   Beloved, let us love one another, for love is from God, and whoever loves has been born of God and knows God

God's love then awakens a response in those who receive it. God loves through believers, who can then act as channels for His love. Christians are branches who must abide in the vine if they are to have that love. We have the assurance that we have passed from death to life because we love others.

I John 3:14   We know that we have passed out of death into life, because we love the brothers. Whoever does not love abides in death.

Once we have received God's love as his children, He expects us to love. In fact, "Whoever does not love does not know God, because God is love" (I John 4:8).

DISCUSSION QUESTIONS:

1 – Is it possible for God to do an unloving thing?

2 – In light of Isaiah 49:15, is it possible for a person, without the influence of God on their life, to actually love?

3 – In light of I John 3:14, how significant is it for us to love one another as Christians?

11 THE COMMANDS TO LOVE

WE ARE COMMANDED TO LOVE GOD WITH ALL THAT WE HAVE

Deuteronomy 6:5   You shall love the Lord your God with all your heart and with all your soul and with all your might.

Matthew 22:35-38   And one of them, a lawyer, asked him a question to test him. 36 "Teacher, which is the great commandment in the Law?" 37 And he said to him, "You shall love the Lord your God with all your heart and with all your soul and with all your mind. 38 This is the great and first commandment.

We are commanded to love God with all of our heart, soul, mind and might. That is pretty much everything we have to love with. Our love to God is meant to be a response to Him from our entire person, with our whole capacity. Why is such a huge demand placed on us to love God? In Deuteronomy chapter six, the people of Israel are about to enter into the promised land. In order for the Israelites to flourish in this land, they must obey the statutes and commandments of God. If they are to succeed and grow and be blessed by all that the land offers, they must fear God and obey His laws (Deuteronomy 6:1-3). But no matter how hard they try to obey and follow the law, without a strong love for God, they will fail. Their love for God is the strength that they need to successfully obey Him. They must understand that God is the only god (Deuteronomy 6:4). There is only one true God, and no other. Unless they have a strong connection to Him through love, they will fall to the level of the other people in the land and worship other gods. Unless they love Him with everything they have got, their affections are likely to wander. This commandment to love God is a commandment for our good. It is a rescuing statute. It is meant to strengthen us to succeed in obedience.

> *John 14:21   Whoever has my commandments and keeps them, he it is who loves me. And he who loves me will be loved by my Father, and I will love him and manifest myself to him."*

I John 4:20-21   If anyone says, "I love God," and hates his brother, he is a liar; for he who does not love his brother whom he has seen cannot love God whom he has not seen. 21 And this commandment we have from him: whoever loves God must also love his brother.

On the one hand, loving God has the effect of helping, or enabling, or improving our obedience. On the other hand, our obedience to God is the very thing that serves to prove our love for Him. Just as the profound obedience of Jesus, which was obedience to the point of death, proved God's love for us, the Lord asks for such proof of our love for Him.

Philippians 2:5-8   Have this mind among yourselves, which is yours in Christ Jesus, 6 who, though he was in the form of God, did not count equality with God a thing to be grasped, 7 but emptied himself, by taking the form of a servant, being born in the likeness of men. 8 And being found in human form, he humbled himself by becoming obedient to the point of death, even death on a cross.

What is involved in our love for God? How is our love for God proven and demonstrated? In absolute, slave-like obedience to His commands (John 14:21). In our love for our brothers in the Lord (I John 4:20). And through humility – emptying ourselves, and taking on the form of servants (Philippians 2:7).

We are to obey to the extreme. During the wedding at Cana of Galilee, the host ran out of wine. Mary, the Lord's mother, asked Jesus to fix the problem. Her sage advice to the servants who would witness the water being turned into wine was simple and yet profound; "Do whatever He tells you" (John 2:5). And they responded by obeying to the extreme. When Jesus told them to fill the water pots with water, what did they do? They filled them up all the way to the very brim (John 2:7). Now, the servants might have heard this command to fill the water pots with water, then looked at each other with quizzical looks, and said to the Lord, "we don't need water, we need wine." Or they might have thought, "we should be using our time raising funds to buy more wine, and you want us to waste our time going back and forth from the well to the water pots all day long carrying heavy buckets of water? But again. Mary, the mother of Jesus gave the servants some very good advice. She said, "Do whatever He tells you." Good to see that she had learned as His earthly mother that it was a wise thing to do whatever He tells you. We also, should take her advice to our hearts and never question Him, but obey without hesitation. It may not always seem that His commands have much to do with the situation. Like the hard labor of filling water pots with water when what is needed is wine. But remember, it is through the command, and through obedience to the command that the miracle of the blessing will come. There is a connection between the water and the wine, even if we do not see it. There is a connection, and sometimes you just have to trust Him that there is a connection between the need and what He is commanding you to do. Sometimes His command may seem just plain crazy. Like the time that Peter and his crew had been fishing all night long without catching anything. Jesus told him, "Put your nets down into the water right over there." Peter said, "we've been fishing there all night with no luck, but if you tell me to try there again, I will." And they caught so many fish they couldn't even carry them all in one boat! In obedience, we are both blessed and our love for God is verified.

Our love for God is also verified in our love for one another as believers. "Whoever loves God must also love his brother." If we do not love each other while at the same time we claim to love God, John says that we are liars. It is just not possible that the same heart that genuinely loves God would be able to hate his fellow Christians. How do we love our brothers in such a way that our love for

God is validated? We look upon them as being more important than ourselves (Philippians 2:3). We spend some of our heart's effort on meeting their needs and not just our own (Philippians 2:4). We lay down our life for their sake and for their good (John 15:13, Philippians 2:17).

OUR LOVE IS EASILY MISDIRECTED

Romans 1:24-25   Therefore God gave them up in the lusts of their hearts to impurity, to the dishonoring of their bodies among themselves, 25 because they exchanged the truth about God for a lie and worshiped and served the creature rather than the Creator, who is blessed forever! Amen.

Luke 14:26   If anyone comes to me and does not hate his own father and mother and wife and children and brothers and sisters, yes, and even his own life, he cannot be my disciple.

Our love is easily misdirected by loving creation rather than the creator. It loses sight of the eternal for the temporal. It focuses on the self, often to the exclusion of God and others. We become idolaters, focusing a part or all of our love elsewhere. We are "love breakers" as much as we are "law breakers."

Genesis chapter twenty-two presents a classic struggle: the conflicting pulls of love. Abraham loves Isaac, the child of God's promise, and Abraham loves God as well. But God tests his heart, to see which love will control his actions. For the sake of the love of God, Abraham is willing to sacrifice the son he loves. His response is to a greater love. Jesus describes this conflict as hating others in order to love and follow God.

Idolatry is the simple act of loving someone or something more than we love God. Our love for God is to be our primary love, to which all other loves must bow and serve. Of course, the Lord doesn't mean that we are to literally hate anyone. But He means that relative to our love for God, our love for any other must be secondary. To do otherwise is to be guilty of idolatry.

WE ARE COMMANDED TO LOVE OUR NEIGHBOR AS OURSELVES

Matthew 22:37-40 And he said to him, "You shall love the Lord your God with all your heart and with all your soul and with all your mind. 38 This is the great and first commandment. 39 And a second is like it: You shall love your neighbor as yourself. 40 On these two commandments depend all the Law and the Prophets."

"Love Your Neighbor as Yourself." Love for neighbor is a decision that we make to treat others with respect and concern, to put the interests of our neighbors on a level with our own interests. It demands a practical outworking in everyday life. The Old Testament talks about several practical things you can do for your neighbors.

> *Deuteronomy 22:8* "*When you build a new house, you shall make a parapet for your roof, that you may not bring the guilt of blood upon your house, if anyone should fall from it.*

One practical, biblical way to love your neighbor is to make your house safe for visitors. Build a fence around the roof to keep people from falling off. Don't let your actions bring harm to others. That is a pretty basic way to love your neighbors. Do not hurt them!

> *Deuteronomy 24:6* *No one shall take a mill or an upper millstone in pledge, for that would be taking a life in pledge.*

Another practical, biblical way to love your neighbor is when you loan them money, don't take something they need on a daily basis as collateral.

Don't take away their ability to grind grain and prepare meals. Don't mess with someone's ability to make a living. Don't be tyrannical. Don't be overbearing. Don't smother someone over whom you have some power. Don't use your financial power over another person to your advantage and to their harm.

> *Leviticus 19:9-10   "When you reap the harvest of your land, you shall not reap your field right up to its edge, neither shall you gather the gleanings after your harvest. 10 And you shall not strip your vineyard bare, neither shall you gather the fallen grapes of your vineyard. You shall leave them for the poor and for the sojourner: I am the Lord your God.*

Allow the poor to glean leftovers from your orchards and fields. Don't be selfish. Don't demand the right to take all that is even rightfully yours. Be generous and share. The lack of love is no more clearly expressed than in the closed hand to other's needs.

> *I John 3:17   But if anyone has the world's goods and sees his brother in need, yet closes his heart against him, how does God's love abide in him?*

If there is someone with a need that you see,

if anyone has a need that you are aware of, and you have the goods, you have the means to do something for them, but you close your heart, then something is wrong. The question is how does God's love abide in the one who does that? The answer is that it does not.

> *James 2:14-17   What good is it, my brothers, if someone says he has faith but does not have works? Can that faith save him? 15 If a brother or sister is poorly clothed and lacking in daily food, 16 and one of you says to them, "Go in peace, be warmed and filled," without giving them the things needed for the body, what good is that? 17 So also faith by itself, if it does not have works, is dead.*

> *I John 3:18   Little children, let us not love in word or talk but in deed and in truth.*

Don't say that you love, do it! Love with actions. Don't say "go in peace, be warmed and filled," but actually give them warmth and food. When it comes to love, doing is more important than saying.

> *I Peter 4:8   Above all, keep loving one another earnestly, since love covers a multitude of sins.*

Love also protects the loved one, even in their wrong doing and guilt. The active love of brothers and sisters in the Lord covers a multitude of sins. It does not expose sins. It does not gossip about sins. It quickly forgives and forgets.

Our actions illustrate our love. Love for neighbor is "love in action," doing something specific and tangible for others. The New Testament concept closely parallels that of the Old Testament. John writes: "Dear children, let us not love with words or tongue but with actions and in truth." Believers need to share with those in need, whether that need is for food, water, lodging, clothing, healing, or friendship.

Matthew 25:34-40   Then the King will say to those on his right, 'Come, you who are blessed by my Father, inherit the kingdom prepared for you from the foundation of the world. 35 For I was hungry and you gave me food, I was thirsty and you gave me drink, I was a stranger and you welcomed me, 36 I was naked and you clothed me, I was sick and you visited me, I was in prison and you came to me.' 37 Then the righteous will answer him, saying, 'Lord, when did we see you hungry and feed you, or thirsty and give you drink? 38 And when did we see you a stranger and welcome you, or naked and clothe you? 39 And when did we see you sick or in prison and visit you?' 40 And the King will answer them, 'Truly,

I say to you, as you did it to one of the least of these my brothers, you did it to me.'

There is an emotional aspect to loving people in these ways, but the needs are also very practical. Love is demonstrated by feeding others, by giving a drink, by being welcoming and hospitable toward people, by seeing to their practical needs and visiting them. The love demonstrated in the parable of the good Samaritan shows that the love being talked about is not simply an emotional response to someone's plight, but is a practical response to someone who is in need.

The command to love others is based on how God has loved us. Since believers have been the recipients of love, they must also love. Since Christ has laid down his life for us, we must be willing to lay down our lives for our brothers.

Many people in Jesus' day believed that a neighbor was a fellow Israelite. When asked to define who a neighbor was, however, Jesus told the parable of the good Samaritan. The good Samaritan was a person who knowingly crossed traditional boundaries to help a wounded Jew (Luke 10:29-37). So a neighbor is not just someone like me, or someone in my particular group or category. A neighbor is anyone who is in need. Jesus also told his disciples that a "neighbor" might even be someone who hates them, curses them, or mistreats them. The Old Testament charge was to "love your neighbor as yourself" (Leviticus 19:18). But Jesus gave his disciples a new command with a new and different motive: "Love each other as I have loved you" (John 15:12). Paul affirms that "the entire law is summed up in a single command: Love your neighbor as yourself" (Galatians 5:14). James sees the command to love one another as a "royal law" (James 2:8). Love is even the motivation for evangelism. Christ's love compels us to become ambassadors for Christ, with the ministry of reconciliation (II Corinthians 5:14).

WE ARE COMMANDED TO LOVE OUR ENEMIES

Luke 6:27   But I say to you who hear, Love your enemies, do good to those who hate you,

Continue reading in Luke chapter six, and you see this love of enemies made more specific. Do good to those who hate you. To the one who hits your cheek, offer him the other one as well. Bless those who curse you. Pray for those who abuse you. If they take away your cloak, give them your tunic too. Give to everyone who begs from you. If someone takes your goods, don't ask to have them back. As you wish others would do to you, do so to them. If you love those who love you, how does that set you apart? Even sinners do that. If you lend money only to the ones you know will pay you back, how does that set you apart from the world? But lend expecting nothing back, and your reward will be great! Then you will be sons of God, because He is kind to the ungrateful and to the evil. So you ought to be merciful like He is merciful.

To love an enemy is culturally radical and personally very challenging. It requires you to surrender the love for fairness you might have. In order to actually do it, you have to come to terms with the idea that you can live with receiving less favorable treatment than you give to others. You must become more willing to endure and sustain one-sided relationships. But when you grasp the truth that that is exactly what God does for us, it becomes more doable.

DISCUSSION QUESTIONS:

1 – What does it mean to love God with each of these parts of you; heart, soul, mind and might?

2 – In what practical way can you love your non-Christian neighbors?

3 - What will it take for you to love an enemy?

12 THE WAY OF LOVE
(I CORINTHIANS 13)

1 The Emptiness Of Religion Without Love

GIFTS AND ABILITIES WITHOUT LOVE

I Corinthians 13:1   If I speak in the tongues of men and of angels, but have not love, I am a noisy gong or a clanging cymbal.

The Corinthians seem like people who were impressed by the exercise of the spiritual gifts. To them, it was a way of measuring the spirituality of people. If, for example, someone could speak in tongues or if they excelled in some other gift, they were worthy of honor. But Paul tries to bring their way of assessing people back to the Christian and godly basics. Jesus had said that the most important commandment was to love God with all you have, and the second most important commandment was to love your neighbor as yourself. In fact, the commandment to love is so important that without it anything else one may do in the way of exercising spiritual gifts is empty, meaningless and without reward from God. No matter how greatly one is gifted, without love they are just making a lot of empty noise. Paul, before he knew the Lord, was greatly gifted and highly educated, but he was clearly not a person who knew how to love. He was in fact hateful, even violently so.

> *Acts 7:58   Then they cast him out of the city and stoned him. And the witnesses laid down their garments at the feet of a young man named Saul.*

> *Acts 8:1-3   And there arose on that day a great persecution against the church in Jerusalem, and they were all scattered throughout the regions of Judea and Samaria, except the apostles. 2 Devout men buried Stephen and made great lamentation over him. 3 But Saul was ravaging the church, and entering house after house, he dragged off men and women and committed them to prison*

Paul was with the men who stoned Stephen to death. He was a companion in their sin. That day was the beginning of a great and sustained persecution against the early church. And Saul played a large role in that persecution. He is described as one who was "ravaging the church, breaking into the homes of believers and dragging them off to prison." While other men were courageously and lovingly burying their beloved Stephen, Saul was busy ravaging and dragging off more victims. Saul's religion was not a religion of love. It was violently legalistic and controlling. So even though he was a very gifted and educated man, without love he was only like a loud, droning, uncomfortable noise. Without love, his great academic gifting was vindictive, punishing and not in any way healing or refreshing.

RELIGIOUS POWER WITHOUT LOVE

> *I Corinthians 13:2   And if I have prophetic powers, and understand all mysteries and all knowledge, and if I have all faith, so as to remove mountains, but have not love, I am nothing.*

To have prophetic powers is a very big gift. To understand all mysteries and all knowledge is even bigger. What a great Bible teacher, what a phenomenal preacher you could be with such knowledge and understanding! But even these awesome powers are meaningless without love.

However much of a "something" a person who has these powers might think they are, without love, they are nothing.

We know that we are saved through faith alone, in Christ alone (Ephesians 2:8-9, 3:9, Romans 4:5, 5:1). This might lead us to conclude that faith is the basic currency of salvation. But we also know that faith alone by itself is not sufficient.

> *James 2:14-17   What good is it, my brothers, if someone says he has faith but does not have works? Can that faith save him? 15 If a brother or sister is poorly clothed and lacking in daily food, 16 and one of you says to them, "Go in peace, be warmed and filled," without giving them the things needed for the body, what good is that? 17 So also faith by itself, if it does not have works, is dead.*

Faith must be accompanied by works in order to be legitimate faith. To have faith in God without love is a contradiction, because all who come to truly "know" the Lord in salvation become like Him in love. It is not that something we do must be added to what Jesus has already done. What He did on the cross is all that is needed for our salvation. But if you are not a person who "does" what you can when a need arrises in front of you, then the authenticity of your faith is in serious question.

Faith without active love is not saving faith. A disciple who does not become like Jesus in love, is not a true disciple.

SACRIFICE WITHOUT LOVE

I Corinthians 13:3   If I give away all I have, and if I deliver up my body to be burned, but have not love, I gain nothing.

God pays attention to our motives, and it is possible to do great things without the right motive, which then makes them meaningless things in the light of eternity. You can go all the way up to the point of giving your life, even without love, having some other motivation, and to God your sacrifice is meaningless. We see this all throughout human history. How many men have bravely given their lives on battle fields around the globe for ungodly causes and for ungodly leaders? Far too many to count. God is not easily impressed and He cannot be faked out. Is it possible for us to sometimes do things that are good things, but to have a deeper purpose behind them that is not a loving purpose? Certainly, it is possible, and it is likely that it happens often. Jesus said that there is no greater love than when a man lays down his life for his friends. But great sacrifice without love is something else altogether. There are many other motives for sacrifice besides love. And all of those other motives are in some way self-centered.

2 What Love Is And Does

LOVE IS PATIENT AND KIND

I Corinthians 13:4a   Love is patient and kind

The prophet Hosea obeyed the command of the Lord and married a woman who would be a prostitute. He displayed great patience in continuing to love her, accept her, forgive her, find her when she strayed from him to other men, and even pay money to get her out of the troubles she got herself into. The Lord demonstrated His patient love through Hosea's life. Love is patient and kind. Love has the patience to endure long trials of being wronged and underappreciated. Love can endure a lot from people because it is based on our love for God. And our love for God is a response to His incredible patience with us. Love has a kind sensitivity to the suffering of others. Love can act with incredible acts of kindness on behalf of those who are suffering – even if their suffering is brought about by their own poor decisions. Christian love has this kind of patient kindness because it is a reflection of God's patient kindness toward us.

LOVE IS NOT SELF-PROMOTING

I Corinthians 13:4b-5a   love does not envy or boast; it is not arrogant or rude

Love doesn't envy. It doesn't become unhappy because of someone else's gift or success. It doesn't crave what others have been given, but can be joyful over someone else's blessing. Love doesn't need to be the one who is directly blessed in order to have joy in the blessing. Love can readily rejoice in the happiness of others, even when the same blessing is not personally gained.

Love does not boast. It doesn't try to claim it is in any way better than others. It doesn't brag about its own religiousness and make efforts to be admired. Love is not rude. It doesn't treat others with contempt or belittlement.

LOVE IS NOT SELF-CENTERED

I Corinthians 13:5b   It does not insist on its own way

Love does not demand that the world around

me must conform to the way I like and do things. Love does not put pressure on the loved one to be exactly what I want them to be. Love does not find it difficult to be the one who is not preferred. Love has no problem doing what the other one wants to do, rather than what I may want to do. Love is never about "me," but is always about the one who is being loved by me.

LOVE IS NOT SELF-SENSITIVE

I Corinthians 13:5c   it is not irritable or resentful

Love is not selfish enough to become irritated by others. It does not demand that others do everything they can to make me comfortable. Love is not easily annoyed or easily made angry. Love doesn't get exasperated with others or resent them. Love can endure a lot of wrong without desiring revenge or demanding any recompence.

LOVE LOVES TRUTH & RIGHTEOUSNESS

I Corinthians 13:6   it does not rejoice at wrongdoing, but rejoices with the truth.

Love does not join in with any celebration of

wrong doing. Love rejoices only in the truth; not in wrong, not in lies. If the one you are loving wants you to celebrate or praise their wrong doing, you cannot do that. Love for them dictates that you don't celebrate their wrong doing. The reason that this is a loving attitude is because all "immoral" behavior has terribly negative consequences. And love cannot rejoice over a loved one bringing such consequences upon themself. This godly love is truer than any worldly affirming love that leaves the "loved" one exposed to judgement and wrath without a warning.

LOVE CAN HANDLE A LOT

I Corinthians 13:7a   Love bears all things

Love can handle a lot of bad behavior from the loved one. Love can bear another's faults without becoming resentful. Love can endure a lot of unfair treatment without anger or self-pity. Love can seek the forgiveness and the spiritual well-being of the ones who are crucifying it. From the cross, Jesus Christ sought the forgiveness of those who were killing Him.

LOVE HAS FAITH FOR OTHERS

I Corinthians 13:7b   believes all things

When your loved one is still not serving the Lord, when they are still living in sin, you keep having faith for them. You keep believing what God can do in them, because our God is the God of all mercy. When they cannot have faith for themselves, the one who loves them has faith for them. I have seen this play out hundreds of times, as mothers and other friends and family members continue to pray, day after day, for the salvation of loved ones.

LOVE KEEPS HOPING FOR THE GOOD OF OTHERS

I Corinthians 13:7c   hopes all things

The same idea; we hope for and believe for better things for the ones we love. Current conditions do not put limits on our hope for those whom we love. We remember that we were once strangers to the mercy and forgiveness of the Lord, and yet He brought us out of our utterly hopeless condition and into His marvelous light.

LOVE SURVIVES TRIALS

I Corinthians 13:7d   endures all things

Love can be ignored. Love can be rejected. Love can be taken advantage of. Love can be openly spurned, and yet still be there when it is needed. Love can endure all things because its greater desire is for the eternal good of the ones who are loved. It isn't caught up in its own temporal condition, but sacrificially seeks the eternal good of the other.

LOVE IS FOREVER

I Corinthians 13:8-12   Love never ends. As for prophecies, they will pass away; as for tongues, they will cease; as for knowledge, it will pass away. 9 For we know in part and we prophesy in part, 10 but when the perfect comes, the partial will pass away. 11 When I was a child, I spoke like a child, I thought like a child, I reasoned like a child. When I became a man, I gave up childish ways. 12 For now we see in a mirror dimly, but then face to face. Now I know in part; then I shall know fully, even as I have been fully known.

Many of the things we know today will not last. We will not continue in these bodies on this earth. Human knowledge will vanish under the dust of time. Prophecy and preaching will even disappear. One day we will find ourselves in a very different, very new heaven and very new earth, where nothing which once was remains the same. Many of the things of today will be gone, but one thing will remain – love.

LOVE IS THE BEST

> I Corinthians 13:13 So now faith, hope, and love abide, these three; but the greatest of these is love.

When weighed against the quality of all other things, love will stand out as the greatest thing. Love is the one thing that makes all other good things possible. Love is God and God is love. Love is our hope and our salvation. So we must be people of love.

DISCUSSION QUESTIONS:

1 – Describe how it is possible to be religious without loving. Give examples.

2 – Why is it that love cannot be jealous or envious?

3 – Why can you continue to have faith and hope for someone who has repeatedly made bad decisions?

13 JOY VS HAPPINESS

Galatians 5:22-24   But the fruit of the Spirit is love, joy, peace, patience, kindness, goodness, faithfulness, 23 gentleness, self-control; against such things there is no law. 24 And those who belong to Christ Jesus have crucified the flesh with its passions and desires.

I am not Presbyterian, but I love the Westminster catechism. And question number one is relevant for the subject of joy. Question 1: What is the chief and highest end of man? Answer 1: Man's chief and highest end is to glorify God, and fully to enjoy Him forever. Our end or our purpose - our ultimate destiny sounds so good to me. To glorify God and to enjoy Him forever! Of course, there is the responsibility part, bringing glory to God. We are called upon to live in such a way that His name is not damaged, but is elevated. This can be challenging - at least while we remain in these human bodies with all of their fallen proclivities and desires. But there is also this whole undeserved reward part of enjoying God forever. The Bible tells us that at His right hand there are pleasures forevermore (Psalm 16:11). He calls the place where we will be with Him, paradise (Luke 23:43). Jesus promised us that He, Himself is preparing a place for us (John 14:2-3). And you know I have seen some pretty spectacular places built and prepared by men, but just imagine what kind of amazing place our Lord could build and prepare.

But enjoying Him is not limited to the far distant post-resurrection future. He says in Mark chapter ten (I am paraphrasing), "even if you lose family, friends and property because you are following me, you will get back a hundred-fold now in this life time, of family friends and rewards." Not only is there joy at the end, but there is even plenty of joy to be had in the here and now.

The fruit of the Spirit is joy. If we want to define joy we can look to dictionaries. Here is an example; from the Oxford dictionary, joy is defined as "a feeling of great pleasure and happiness." But when we are thinking about the joy of the Lord, this definition just doesn't feel quite right, does it? It doesn't feel right because our joy seems to run deeper than the word "feeling." A feeling of great pleasure and happiness can come from things that are so much less than God. It doesn't seem right to define the joy we receive from Him with such shallow words. The joy of the Lord runs deeper than those words can describe. This way of defining joy puts it into the place of depending on feelings and circumstances. And we who know the Lord understand that our joy in Him is somehow disconnected from anything that can happen to us in this life. We understand that our joy in the Lord is made of such permanent stuff that the feeble winds of this world's troubles just can't blow it away. Paul calls this world's problems and difficulties "light afflictions." Even though our troubles can feel very heavy, relative to the weight of our joy in the Lord, they are much lighter.

> *II Corinthians 4:16-18   So we do not lose heart. Though our outer self is wasting away, our inner self is being renewed day by day. 17 For this light momentary affliction is preparing for us an eternal weight of glory beyond all comparison, 18 as we look not to the things that are seen but to the things that are unseen. For the things that are seen are transient, but the things that are unseen are eternal.*

Although our outer self is wasting away, our inner self is being continually renewed, refreshed and made whole. I think we grasp somehow that there is a difference between the happiness that can be taken away by adverse circumstances and the joy we know through the Lord.

As I was doing research about joy, I encountered some disagreement among great theological minds on this idea of differentiating happiness and joy. Randy Alcorn has written a book called "Happiness." Do you know Randy Alcorn? If you have any questions about how Christians ought to handle money, he is the guy I have found to be the most enlightening about that. In his book, "Happiness," he has a chapter that focuses on saying that happiness and joy are not really different things in the Bible, and so he would not make any distinction. But I also read an R.C. Sproul article on the subject, and he does think that making a distinction between the two is helpful. So, I will go with R.C. on this one. The word happiness is related to the older English word happenstance, which means that what has happened depended on random chance. In other words, what made me happy depended on a random happening. It was just happenstance that I happened to be there and be made happy by what happened. So then, happiness depends on what happens. "I was so happy that my team won the game." "I was so happy that it didn't rain today." I think that the joy of the Lord cannot be defined as depending on circumstances in the immediate sense. Our joy **does not** depend on what happens today. Here is what the Lord Himself says about our joy in Him.

> *John 15:9-11   As the Father has loved me, so have I loved you. Abide in my love. 10 If you keep my commandments, you will abide in my love, just as I have kept my Father's commandments and abide in his love. 11 These things I have spoken to you, that my joy may be in you, and that your joy may be full.*

So then, His joy being in us, and His joy in us being the fullest joy it can be does depend on something. It depends on us abiding, or remaining in His love. And it also seems to be related to our obedience to Him. Obeying His commands is what causes us to abide in His love, and abiding in His love is what brings the joy. So our joy then is not dependent on the happenstance that causes pleasure or happiness, but is much more connected to our relationship with the Lord, as our Lord, whom we obey and follow.

Our joy then could be said to be more related to what we believe and who we are in Jesus, than it is related to what happens to us. As people who have been given a new heart, we are transformed into the kind of people who know we are loved by Him and who desire to follow and obey Him and love Him back as much as possible. And it is such an intense transformation that we are almost removed from what happenstance brings us. Happiness depends on circumstances. Happiness comes from what happens. Happiness and pleasure rely on happenstance.

Joy does not depend on circumstances. How can that be true? Because joy depends on something that never changes. It can't be lessened by anything that happens. Joy in the Lord cannot be hampered by souring human relationships. Joy in the Lord cannot be lessened by financial difficulties. Joy in the Lord can't be broken by bad health, bad weather, or anything else. Joy comes from God Himself, and God never changes, so our joy in Him never changes either.

But if we are living without the awareness of what God has done for us, we can know pleasure, we can know occasional happiness, but we cannot know true joy. Because joy has only one source, and that is God. Joy comes from a direct, personal, continuing connection to God. Without that relationship it is impossible to know true joy.

So, if we are to make a distinction between the joy of the Lord and other kinds of pleasure and happiness, we would have to say that the difference comes from what it is based in. The distinction is in the source of it all. Is the source of our good feelings in temporal happenstance, or is the source of our good feelings in the eternal promises of God?

DISCUSSION QUESTIONS:

1 – How is it possible to have both disappointment in circumstances and joy in the Lord at the same time?

2 – Is it possible to have true joy without having an eternal perspective?

3 – Which qualities or attributes of God do you find joy in?

14 THE SOURCE OF JOY

John 15:11   These things I have spoken to you, that my joy may be in you, and that your joy may be full.

I Peter 1:8   Though you have not seen him, you love him. Though you do not now see him, you believe in him and rejoice with joy that is inexpressible and filled with glory,

Our joy comes from Jesus. This joy arrives in our hearts when we hear and receive His words. "These things I have spoken to you, that my joy may be in you, and that your joy may be full" (John 15:11). The first believers where there with the Lord. They heard Him speak those words that brought them joy. We, however, have not seen Him and have not heard His words directly spoken from His mouth to our literal ears. But even without directly seeing Him or hearing Him, we love Him and are filled with His joy through the written and preached word that He has provided for us. We can be filled with an amazing joy when we grasp just what he has done for us. When we truly understand our sin and how awful it is, and when we truly understand our Savior and how incredible He is, then there is nothing for us to do but be filled with thankfulness and joy at what is in store for us. In knowing Jesus, there is available to us great joy – a permanent satisfaction. This is how I would define the Joy of the Lord; this Joy is a permanent satisfaction. It is a satisfaction which cannot be reduced or eradicated. In this world there are many sources of temporary satisfaction, but no sources of permanent satisfaction. It is difficult to break the human habit of looking for satisfaction from other sources. But this is one of our goals in understanding the joy of the Lord, to break the habit of seeking our joy in other things.

1 – A Woman Who Looked For Satisfaction From Relationships

In John chapter four we read about the Lord's encounter with the Samaritan woman at the well. He invites her to ask Him for living water in verse ten, saying, "If you knew the gift of God, and who it is that is saying to you, 'Give me a drink,' you would have asked him, and he would have given you living water." All she has to do is ask for this living water, this eternal life, and He says He will give it to her. It is such an easy thing to simply ask, anyone can do it. But she has some doubts about what He can do.

> *John 4:11-12   The woman said to him, "Sir, you have nothing to draw water with, and the well is deep. Where do you get that living water? 12 Are you greater than our father Jacob? He gave us the well and drank from it himself, as did his sons and his livestock."*

She says to the Lord, "you have nothing to draw water with, and the well is pretty deep, how are you going to give me living water?" She doesn't quite understand yet who it is she is talking to. She is still thinking in a material way about water. Which means that they are not yet talking about the same kind of water. So, the Lord answers her.

> *John 4:13-15   Jesus said to her, "Everyone who drinks of this water will be thirsty again, 14 but whoever drinks of the water that I will give him will never be thirsty again. The water that I will give him will become in him a spring of water welling up to eternal life." 15 The woman said to him, "Sir, give me this water, so that I will not be thirsty or have to come here to draw water."*

Jesus said to her, "everyone who drinks of this water will be thirsty again." Meaning that the place of need in mankind is far too deep for the waters of earth to quench. The dryness in the human soul is caused by a spiritual thirst. Even if a person could reach down to discover and drink the deepest waters that the earth has to offer, he would still soon be thirsty again. People may take their fill of pleasure in what this world has to offer, yet it will fail to satisfy for very long. They may indulge in every comfort and luxury that money can buy, and still wind up feeling empty inside. They may enjoy the favor of those around them, they may become famous and be honored and admired by crowds of fawning fans, and still go to bed with an empty, aching dissatisfaction deep down at the core of their being. They may be intellectually inclined and get to study all the science, philosophy, religion and everything under the sun, like Solomon, and yet find it all worth nothing in the end. There ought to be signs placed over all the various kinds of wells of water that this world offers, warning that they will not satisfy. Every earthly well needs to have a sign that says, "Whoever drinks of this water will thirst again, so don't bother drinking here."

Now she sees that what He is offering her, the living water, is something that brings a permanent satisfaction. All that she has chased after in her life up to this point have been things that can provide only a fleeting satisfaction. They can quench your thirst, but all too soon the thirst returns. All other sources of happiness or joy are like earthly water, it satisfies only for a little while. And she wants this permanent satisfaction. She wants this joy that cannot be taken away from her. She wants it, and now she takes Jesus up on His offer and she asks for the living water. And now that she has asked for it, He will lead her in the way that she can get it.

> *John 4:16-18   Jesus said to her, "Go, call your husband, and come here." 17 The woman answered him, "I have no husband." Jesus said to her, "You are right in saying, 'I have no husband'; 18 for you have had five husbands, and the one you now have is not your husband. What you have said is true.*

He answers her with an amazing answer. He answers her with a mixture of truth and grace. He says, "go, call your husband and come here." By saying go and get your husband, He is forcing her to stand before Him transparently. He is making her reveal her soul's nakedness and shame. He leads her to confess her sin. Two things the Lord tells her to do: the first was kind of solemn and searching; the second, though, was gracious and inviting. "Go," He said, "call your husband." That was a word designed to bring her to repentance, to bring her to the realization also that the way that she has been trying to quench her thirst wasn't working. "And come here," that was a word of grace for her. The force of what He said was this: If you really want this living water which I have been telling you about, you can obtain it only as a poor, convicted, contrite sinner. Come back to me as that sinner who understands the evil and the futility of drinking from the well you have been drinking from, and then I will give you the water that truly satisfies, with a permanent satisfaction. Not only did He say "Go," but He added "Come." She was not only to go and call her husband, but she was to come back to Jesus in her true character and condition. It was a beautiful mingling of "grace" and "truth." Truth which required her to come out into the light as a self-confessed sinner; grace which invited her to return to the Lord and receive the living water that satisfies forever and ever.

She had had five husbands and was now with another man whom she was not married to. She had hoped that a relationship would bring her that deeper satisfaction, that joy that she longed for. But every one of her relationships came to an unsatisfying end – divorce. Where she found her true and lasting joy was in being transparent before the Lord in repentance, in forsaking the empty wells that didn't satisfy, and coming to Him for the water that does satisfy forever, permanently.

2 – A Man Who Looked For Satisfaction From Money

There was another person who encountered Jesus and had his way of looking for satisfaction changed forever. Zacchaeus the tax collector loved money. He believed with all he had that money would bring him joy and happiness, so he went about getting more and more money. His determination to get more money was so great that it even led him to betray his own people to get it. He went to work for the Romans, extracting money from the Jewish people to give to their enemies. And, in the processed, he learned to skim as much off for himself as he could.

> *Luke 19:1-7   He entered Jericho and was passing through. 2 And behold, there was a man named Zacchaeus. He was a chief tax collector and was rich. 3 And he was seeking to see who Jesus was, but on account of the crowd he could not, because he was small in stature. 4 So he ran on ahead and climbed up into a sycamore tree to see him, for he was about to pass that way. 5 And when Jesus came to the place, he looked up and said to him, "Zacchaeus, hurry and come down, for I must stay at your house today." 6 So he hurried and came down and received him joyfully. 7 And when they saw it, they all grumbled, "He has gone in to be the guest of a man who is a sinner."*

In verse five Jesus came to the place where Zacchaeus was. The Lord knows where to find His people. And He knows their names. In fact, He calls them by name to come to Him. He has appointments to meet with all of them. He knows the time and place of each of these appointments, even if His people do not, and He will be there just in time to rescue them. Jesus said to him, "hurry and come down, for I MUST stay at your house today." That is such an amazing, miraculous and merciful moment for the man who loved money. Zacchaeus has an appointment with Jesus that day, and nothing will be permitted to stop it. And being invited to have Jesus come into his house and into his life, Zacchaeus received Him joyfully.

The man, Zacchaeus had been a notorious sinner, stealing from and defrauding his own people. The satisfaction he had hoped to receive from money, though, was coming up empty. It was leaving him with a gnawing feeling of emptiness and disappointment. The Bible doesn't exactly include these details, but I think they are self-evident. When Jesus called him by name and came into his life, a great change took place in the man, Zacchaeus. He received that deeper satisfaction which nothing else could give.

Luke 19:8-10   And Zacchaeus stood and said

> *to the Lord, "Behold, Lord, the half of my goods I*
> *give to the poor. And if I have defrauded anyone*
> *of anything, I restore it fourfold." 9 And Jesus said*
> *to him, "Today salvation has come to this house,*
> *since he also is a son of Abraham. 10 For the Son*
> *of Man came to seek and to save the lost."*

A sign that salvation had come to Zacchaeus was that he no longer cared about money like he used to. He didn't need to care about it anymore because now he had found the source of true and permanent satisfaction.

This joy, which is the fruit of the Holy Spirit is unlike anything which is produced from the natural world in the heart. It is a joy that is completely unique to the regenerated soul. It is different from the ordinary joys of being content and healthy, because it can persist even in times of poverty, weakness, sickness and pain. It is different from those moments of joy that you experience with friends or family when you are having a party or celebration of some kind, because it can continue even when there is no worldly reason to celebrate. It is different from all normal joys, because it is not truly connected to anything in this natural world. And because it is not connected to anything in the natural world, nothing that happens in the natural world can take it away. Poverty cannot take it away. Sickness cannot take it away. Persecution cannot take it away. If your joy can be stolen from you by financial loss, or sickness or persecution, or any other reasons, then you are not experiencing the joy of the Lord. Your joy may have a different source.

In Psalm 34:5, we read, "They looked unto Him and were radiant." Those who look to the Lord become radiant with the joy of the Lord. They glow from being exposed to the brightness of Him who is everything. The joy of the Lord arises from leaving all our burdens at His feet. The joy of the Lord comes from believing that He has forgiven our sins entirely. The joy of the Lord comes from knowing that nothing can come into our lives which God does not send or permit. The joy of the Lord comes from knowing that He is doing all things as wisely and as kindly, and as lovingly in our lives as possible. The joy of the Lord comes from knowing that we have been lifted out of the world of sin and sorrow and death, and are being planted forever into the realm of God's light and love. The joy of the Lord comes from knowing that we have already received eternal life, and we have already begun to live with Him and in Him. The joy of the Lord comes from the fellowship we have with the Lord, even now. It is probably not even possible to faithfully and accurately describe it in human terms. But if you find yourself searching for that one final thing that will complete your joy in life, then you are in the wrong frame of mind, because Jesus is the only one who can be that missing piece. No place, no person, no job, no anything can do for you what the Lord can do for you.

DISCUSSION QUESTIONS:

1 – Where have you searched for joy other than in the Lord? How did that search work out?

2 – Read and talk about Ecclesiastes 1:14.

3 – Discuss the eternal importance of placing your hope in the Lord rather than in any other thing.

15 THE STRENGTH OF JOY

In the book of Nehemiah, we see a revival happen. The book of the Law, the Bible, was read and clearly explained to the people. The revival came from the reading and the clear understanding of the Bible. It was perhaps the first time that many of the people had heard the word preached in such a way that its true meaning was made clear and obvious to them.

Nehemiah 8:7-8   Also Jeshua, Bani, Sherebiah, Jamin, Akkub, Shabbethai, Hodiah, Maaseiah, Kelita, Azariah, Jozabad, Hanan, Pelaiah, the Levites, helped the people to understand the Law, while the people remained in their places. 8 They read from the book, from the Law of God, clearly, and they gave the sense, so that the people understood the reading.

The reading of the word and the giving of the sense of the word (teaching and preaching) are the keys to a revolution in the hearts of God's people. So often we may fail to appreciate the literal power that the preached word has for us who sit under it and hear it with ears to hear. The preached word of God has the power to bring sinners to repentance and salvation. And it has the power to sanctify to the uttermost those believers who faithfully attend its place of preaching. Hebrews 4:12 tells us that "the word of God is living and active, sharper than any two-edged sword, piercing to the division of soul and spirit, of joints and marrow, and discerning the thoughts and intentions of the heart." It is able to pierce down into the deepest part of a person and make a basic, fundamental and systemic change in the heart. It has the power to orient a heart away from evil, selfish sinfulness, and toward godly attitudes, thoughts and behaviors.

> *Nehemiah 8:9   And Nehemiah, who was the governor, and Ezra the priest and scribe, and the Levites who taught the people said to all the people, "This day is holy to the Lord your God; do not mourn or weep." For all the people wept as they heard the words of the Law.*

The first response to hearing and understanding

the words of the law was mourning, sadness, conviction of sin.

> *Nehemiah 8:10-12   Then he said to them, "Go your way. Eat the fat and drink sweet wine and send portions to anyone who has nothing ready, for this day is holy to our Lord. And do not be grieved, for the joy of the Lord is your strength." 11 So the Levites calmed all the people, saying, "Be quiet, for this day is holy; do not be grieved." 12 And all the people went their way to eat and drink and to send portions and to make great rejoicing, because they had understood the words that were declared to them.*

The final result of understanding the word of God was joy. The people made great rejoicing. Their joy followed repentance. Their joy followed the reading of the word. Their joy followed the teaching of the right meaning of the word.

Joy comes from getting right with God. And this joy works as a strength for us, sustaining us through hard times, through griefs, through struggles with health, struggles with other people, struggles with the normal, common woes of this fallen world. The joy of the Lord is your strength because it carries you through the storms of this life.

There are two men who have greatly affected

me in the area of appreciating the joy that the Lord brings. The first man was an old pastor from Washington, Pennsylvania. His name was Michael Sitko, but I just knew him as brother Michael. I was a young pastor in my thirties when I met him, and he was an old, blind man in his mid-seventies. Although he was a pastor, I never heard him preach. I met him through a group of local pastors who used to pray together once in a while. The first time I heard brother Michael pray I was deeply moved and thrilled with excitement at the same time. He prayed with such heart-felt passion to the Lord whom he so obviously loved, that you couldn't help but be affected. His prayer struck a familiar chord in my heart as it helped me know much more thoroughly what I already knew. And that was that our God deserves every bit of our affections and emotions in love. I learned from brother Michael that a much greater and deeper joy was mine to have. And from that point in my life on, my prayer was changed forever.

The other man who profoundly impacted me , and still informs my understanding of the joy of the Lord is John Piper. When you listen to the teachings of Mr. Piper, you can't help but notice that the academic and theological quality of his material is outstanding. And I am certainly drawn to that aspect of his teaching. I always believed that his sound and thorough theological knowledge pervades his teaching in a pure and enlightening way. And that aspect of his ministry clearly has it's pull on me. But that is not the primary thing that draws me back to his ministry over and over again. No, it is his pervasive, unchanging and persistent joy in the Lord that brings me back. And that joy draws me back because I gain strength from it. To be a person who can stand up against the cultural pressures and temptations of the world, you must be a person who knows by real and personal experience, the true joy of the Lord. It is your joy in Him which provides the ability, the spiritual strength, to be like a Joseph who flees from youthful lust. It is the pure joy of the Lord which gives the martyr the power to face death with a resolute certainty that will not compromise just for some temporary relief. It is your joy in the Lord which enables you to pass over all the illegitimate, earthly, soulish sources of joy, to get to the real and pure source of joy. The joy of the Lord is our strength!

DISCUSSION QUESTIONS:

1 – How does being right with God provide you with joy?

2 – How does good teaching which enables you to more clearly understand the meaning of the word of God bring you joy?

3 – How is the joy of the Lord your strength?

16 THE CULTIVATION OF JOY

It is a duty for us to cultivate this joy. We have to use some effort to do this. We have to actively fight against any tendency to murmur and complain. We have to fight against the tendency to find fault with God's dealings with us. We must resist the temptation to depression and melancholy as we would resist the temptation to any form of sin. When the sky is all dark and cloudy, we need to be that one weird person who can see the tiny speck of sunshine and blue sky. We need to rest on the promises of God, being certain that He will win in our lives, and the future will absolutely vindicate the long history of our pain. We have to cultivate a cheerful optimism, and an undaunted hope. We must remember and remind ourselves that our future is absolutely glorious.

Psalm 16:11   You will show me the path of life;

in Your presence is fullness of joy; at Your right hand are pleasures forevermore.

These are beautiful words, and they are "now" words. We do not have to wait until some far distant future for the fulfillment of this beautiful promise. Right here, and right now, as we live in fellowship with Him, we will discover the presence of the Lord through the working of the Holy Spirit in our lives. And this is the source of great and ever flowing joy. It is a fountain of living water that will never run dry. We may not be able to rejoice in our circumstances, but we can always rejoice in Jesus Christ. Jesus is the bread of life. He is the fountain of living waters. He is the one whom our soul loves. He is the one who chases all the shadows away.

There is an obligation upon a Christian to be happy. Let me say it again, there is a responsibility laid upon a Christian to be cheerful! It is not merely an invitation, but it is a command. "Be glad in the Lord and rejoice, you righteous (Psalm 32:11)." "Rejoice in the Lord always; and again, I say, rejoice (Philippians 4:4)." The command to rejoice is as clear of a command of God as the command to love the Lord with all you have. But for believers, it is not so hard to find reasons to rejoice.

DISCUSSION QUESTIONS:

1 - How can we cultivate the joy of the Lord in our lives?

2 – Are there ways in which you struggle to be optimistic and joyful?

3 – Is sadness or depression a sin?

17 FINDING JOY

1 Knowing The Lord And His Salvation

I Peter 1:8-9   Though you have not seen him, you love him. Though you do not now see him, you believe in him and rejoice with joy that is inexpressible and filled with glory, 9 obtaining the outcome of your faith, the salvation of your souls.

Even though we don't see Him, we do "see" Him. We know His heart, we know His love, we know His acts of love toward us in particular. We know His eternal greatness and we eagerly await His soon return. We who know Him know a lot about Him from our first-hand encounters with Him in our own hearts and in His word. The prophet Habakkuk said "I will take joy in the God of my salvation." I am going to be happy and celebrate the fact that I know Him and He has saved me. God takes joy in our salvation (read Luke 15) and so should we. If you want to treat yourself to a moment of joy in your salvation, just read Ephesians 1:3-14. Reading those verses is like taking a shower in joy.

2 The Temporal Provision Of God

Deuteronomy 12:7   And there you shall eat before the Lord your God, and you shall rejoice in all to which you have put your hand, you and your households, in which the Lord your God has blessed you.

An unthankful and complaining attitude is sin. Ingratitude also leads to unhappiness. There is no such thing as an ungrateful happy person. Dissatisfaction with the provision of God brought disaster after disaster on the children of Israel in the wilderness. It is ok to enjoy what He has given us in physical provision, and to be thankful. What is not ok is to love the provision over the provider. Enjoy whatever He has given you and be glad.

3 Communion With God

Romans 8:15   For you did not receive the spirit of slavery to fall back into fear, but you have received the Spirit of adoption as sons, by whom we cry, "Abba! Father!"

If you are a real, sincere Christian, you have felt what communion with God is. You are able to call God Father. Although by sin people are separated from him and can look to him only as an offended Lord and a righteously angry Judge, yet you can rejoice at knowing that you have been adopted into the household of faith, and have received that spirit of adoption whereby you cry, "Abba, Father." And since He is your father, you can humbly pray to Him and let Him know all your troubles. As you hunger and thirst after righteousness, you can go to him and know that you will be filled and satisfied. As you feel yourself weak, you can hope for strength from him. It is especially a privilege to pray to him alone, to commune with him in secret, to enter into your closet and shut the door and pray to your Father which is in secret, and know that your Father which sees in secret himself shall reward you openly. You can pour out there before him your heart's inmost sorrows, your own needs. You can wrestle there alone with your God, for the blessings you need, and know that asking you shall receive. You can confess every sin, of word or deed, of thought or desire, and ask for forgiveness through the Savior in whom you trust. You can pour out your soul there in deep supplication for those you love who don't know Jesus. You can bring their sad case before your God, and implore him to stop them and turn them and rescue and save them. Oh, the privilege of private prayer, the joy and peace that flow to the true believer from personal, spiritual communion with the Father of his spirit!

4 Fellowship With Other Believers

Philippians 4:1   Therefore, my brothers, whom I love and long for, my joy and crown, stand firm thus in the Lord, my beloved.

Paul calls his brothers among the Philippians his joy and his crown.   Paul called the Thessalonians the cause of his joy.   Peter told the believers that he wrote to that nothing made him more joyful than to see them serving the Lord well. In fellowship in the Lord there is great joy.

5 There Is Joy In Sanctification

Psalm 32:10-11   Many are the sorrows of the wicked, but steadfast love surrounds the one who trusts in the Lord. 11 Be glad in the Lord, and rejoice, O righteous, and shout for joy, all you upright in heart!

The Joy of a new nature is too important to be left out. The wicked are miserable with sorrow. Their whole life is one heartache after another anguish. But having been forgiven and having been somewhat transformed is like opening the damn that has held back joy.

> *I John 1:21-22   Beloved, if our heart does not condemn us, we have confidence before God; 22 and whatever we ask we receive from him, because we keep his commandments and do what pleases him.*

Joy and gladness come from being conformed to God's holiness. Hebrews 1:9 says of Jesus, "You have loved righteousness and hated wickedness; therefore God, Your God, has anointed You with the oil of gladness beyond Your companions." Note how righteousness and gladness go together. Again, Satan perpetrates a great lie. He makes us think that real happiness is found in sin, whereas holiness is dull and boring and even melancholy. But God's Word teaches that holiness and happiness are bound together. Sin may give momentary pleasures, but it always wreaks destruction and death. Clearly, a person living in sin could not be happy in God's holy presence. Men love darkness and want to hide from the God who is light, because their deeds are evil (John 3:19-21). When Jonah disobeyed God, he tried to run from God's presence. Adam tried to hide and cover his nakedness. So, the only way to know the joy and gladness that come from God's presence is to know that your sins are forgiven through faith in Jesus Christ and to be walking in obedience to Him.

6 The Word Of God Brings Joy

Jeremiah 15:16   Your words were found, and I ate them, and your words became to me a joy and the delight of my heart, for I am called by your name,
O Lord, God of hosts.

Joy comes from the revelation of scripture to opened eyes and hearts. Psalm 19 and Psalm 119 are great reading on this. Think of Jesus' words, "These things I have spoken to you, that my joy may be in you, and that your joy may be full" (John 15:11). The pathway to joy, then, is to give ourselves maximum exposure to His Word and to let it dwell in us richly (Colossians 3:16). The word of God is joy-food for the joy-hungry soul. There is sweetness in the acquisition of knowledge, especially of spiritual knowledge. God's word is sweeter than honey and the honeycomb (Psalm 19:10). With a meager revelation, compared with ours, David could sing, "I have rejoiced in the way of your testimonies, as much as in all riches (Psalm 119:14);" and, "I rejoice in your word, as one that finds great spoil (Psalm 119:162)," and, "your testimonies have I taken as a heritage for ever—for they are the rejoicing of my heart (Psalm 119:111)."

7 We Can Even Find Joy In Hard Times

Habakkuk 3:17-18   Though the fig tree should not blossom, nor fruit be on the vines, the produce of the olive fail and the fields yield no food, the flock be cut off from the fold and there be no herd in the stalls, 18 yet I will rejoice in the Lord; I will take joy in the God of my salvation.

The thought of joy, even in the midst of what normally makes people sad, is the most amazing part of the Bible's teaching on joy. We have a joy which flows unchanged through the midst of troubles. It may be a paradox; but if there is anything undeniable in Christian experience, it is this. We could call ten thousand witnesses, from the martyr in his chains who is about to face his death, to the sick, poverty-stricken person, dying on his straw bed in the Middle Ages. Christian joy has triumphed over every variety of external distress. And the reason is, that it rests on nothing that is sensual, earthly, or fading. It is a joy which flows from the very head of the body of Christ, and which remains and is full, when other fountains have gone dry. This sustaining power of the joy of the Lord is made evident in history, as every attempt to stamp out Christianity through persecution has instead led to the furtherance of the gospel.

8 Even In Persecution We Can Find Joy

Luke 6:22-23   "Blessed are you when people hate you and when they exclude you and revile you and spurn your name as evil, on account of the Son of Man! 23 Rejoice in that day, and leap for joy, for behold, your reward is great in heaven; for so their fathers did to the prophets.

Here is another Bible paradox – joy in persecution. Luke says that it is a blessing to be hated. He says being excluded from society is a cause for celebration. Being reviled and called evil because of your association with Jesus Christ is a cause for rejoicing. In I Peter chapter four we read that we should rejoice in sufferings and be glad because the end result for us is to be rewarded when His glory is revealed. If we are insulted for the name of Christ we are blessed because that same Spirit of glory will rest on us. The deep, hidden joy of the Lord which exists in too deep of a place for evil men or circumstances to root it out, is the secret to the perseverance of the saints.

DISCUSSION QUESTIONS:

1 – How can fellowship with other believers increase your joy in the Lord?

2 – Has there been a time when the word of God, either by reading it or hearing it preached, has brought to a new and refreshing joy?

3 – How is it possible for suffering or persecution to be a source of joy in the Lord?

18 PEACE DESCRIBED

THE FRUIT OF THE SPIRIT IS PEACE

> *Galatians 5:22-24   But the fruit of the Spirit is love, joy, peace, patience, kindness, goodness, faithfulness, 23 gentleness, self-control; against such things there is no law. 24 And those who belong to Christ Jesus have crucified the flesh with its passions and desires.*

The fruit of the Spirit is peace. Everybody wants peace. The whole world cries for peace. I want peace of mind, many say. Young parents just want some peace and quiet most days. People protest for world peace. They said in the 60's "give peace a chance." And we all learned how to give the peace sign. Everybody wants some kind of peace. We hire policemen to keep the peace. We can go to court before the justice of the peace. When we want someone to be quiet, we ask them to hold their peace. We crave an inner peace. We give the Nobel peace prize to peacemakers. Everybody wants some kind of peace. Peace can be defined as the absence of war or conflict. It is freedom from disturbance. It is tranquility. It is when things are not noisy and out of control. It is when things are calm and worries are not at the forefront of your mind.

But all too often people look for peace in the wrong places. And the world is always offering peace that it cannot deliver. There are many false promises of peace out there. Drugs and alcohol offer peace, but don't truly give it. They just temporarily numb you. Sometimes people hope that a change of scenery will bring peace, so they move to a new city, get a new job, marry a new person. But soon the freshness gives way and the old turmoil returns, because they did not leave the disturbance and unrest behind. They couldn't leave it behind because it is in them. And it goes wherever they go. You cannot escape from yourself.

And somehow the world knows how much people crave this elusive peace. So, the world offers fake remedies. Like snake-oil salesmen, they sell their false peace all over the globe. The business of selling peace to humans is a big business - very profitable. We can read about it in the Bible.

Jeremiah 6:13-14   "For from the least to the

greatest of them, everyone is greedy for unjust gain; and from prophet to priest, everyone deals falsely. 14 They have healed the wound of my people lightly, saying, 'Peace, peace,' when there is no peace.

The world tries to offer a false peace, a fake peace. And I include most religions under the umbrella of the world. Even many iterations of the Christian church would come under that umbrella, because they offer a counterfeit peace. From the least of them to the greatest of them, everyone is greedy for unjust gain. And so they deceive people with offers of peace that is never real peace. The world will numb your pain through drugs, alcohol, distracting physical pleasures, through philosophical trickery and sleight of hand. You can purportedly buy peace from scientology, from Mormonism, from therapy, from all kinds of secular and religious gurus. They may claim to be prophets or priests or special messengers who know special secrets. They may even do some minor good. Verse fourteen says they have healed the wound of my people lightly. They have healed mildly, a little bit, superficially. And they cry peace, peace, but there is no peace. The peace the world offers is always a lie. It is always just some temporary numbing of the inner conflict. The different ways in which the world offers peace can never work because they don't address the real problem, which is this – human beings have no peace because they have sinful, wicked hearts that need to be redeemed. But the peace that God gives is different.

> *John 14:27   Peace I leave with you; my peace I give to you. Not as the world gives do I give to you. Let not your hearts be troubled, neither let them be afraid.*

Jesus said "peace I leave with you; my peace I give to you." What is His peace? His peace is tranquility of soul. It is a calming of the inner conflict that is brought about by the guilt of sin. His peace is awareness of eternal rescue. His peace is everlasting connection with God, forever sonship. His peace is the God-given ability to not let your heart be troubled or afraid by whatever comes your way in life. "I will give you peace that only I can give," Jesus says, "peace I leave with you, my peace." Not the kinds of peace the world gives. Not the kinds of things people always chase after; pleasure, wealth, and fame. These things always leave you with anxiety and even remorse. They cannot meet the eternal needs you have inside of you. They cannot give peace of soul. They promise through false religion and philosophy to give you peace, but they leave you with your sin and your guilt and your sense of coming judgement. "Peace, peace," they cry, but there is no peace.

Peace with God cannot come unless the problem of sin is dealt with. Since the world's offers of peace cannot do that, they are false offers, lies, cons and scams. But the peace that Jesus gives is different. It soothes the soul at the deepest level. It calms the condemning conscience. It remains through the storms. It is even there at the moment of death to bring comfort and hope. His peace is not like the world gives, and the world can't take it away.

When I think of peace as the fruit of the Spirit, I think of three different kinds of peace. There is peace with God. There is peace with others – with other human beings. And there is the peace of God. When the Bible says that the fruit of the Spirit is peace, I think it means the latter one – the peace of God. But, of course, peace with God and peace with others are both connected to the peace of God. The peace of God is only possible after peace with God is made. And the same is true about peace with other people. It is only possible to be at true peace with others after a lasting peace with God is established. So we'll consider all three of those kinds of peace, because they are inseparable really.

DISCUSSION QUESTIONS:

1 – Why do the world's offers of peace leave people disappointed?

2 - In what ways have you sought peace without finding it?

3 – How does sin take away inner peace?

19 PEACE WITH GOD

Peace with God is very important for the individual person; for me, for you, because we are born in a state of war with God. We are born resisting Him, disobeying Him, rejecting Him, running from Him. We are born as people who love the fallen world of sin. And we know what the Bible tells us about people who love the world.

> *James 4:4   You adulterous people! Do you not know that friendship with the world is enmity with God? Therefore. whoever wishes to be a friend of the world makes himself an enemy of God.*

Fallen man finds himself in this state of enmity with God. This is very dangerous, because this means that every unredeemed person on earth is only one heart-beat away from eternal woe, with no relief – ever. And all of these people we see walking around living their lives are completely oblivious to the fact that they are teetering on the edge of disaster. Disaster that there is no coming back from. Peace with God is so vital for everyone. So, when God the Spirit does what only He can do, and He touches a human heart, making it possible for a person to repent and be turned to God, it is the greatest miracle and the most profound moment of that person's life.

> *Romans 5:1-2   Therefore, since we have been justified by faith, we have peace with God through our Lord Jesus Christ. 2 Through him we have also obtained access by faith into this grace in which we stand, and we rejoice in hope of the glory of God.*

"Therefore, since we have been justified, we have peace with God." Peace with God comes through being justified. And having the peace of God flows from being at peace with God. Because as verse two says, by having peace with God we obtain an entryway into His grace. And in His grace, all the things that were once impossible and out of our reach become reality for us.

This peace with God, this reconciliation with God, also provides us with purpose and with duty – which human beings are built to long for. We are created by God, and one of the things He made us with is a desire to do something that is significant and meaningful. We have an innate desire to be part of something much bigger than ourselves. And being at peace with God fulfills this need we have by giving us a mission. We see this mission in...

> *II Corinthians 5:17-20   Therefore, if anyone is in Christ, he is a new creation. The old has passed away; behold, the new has come. 18 All this is from God, who through Christ reconciled us to himself and gave us the ministry of reconciliation; 19 that is, in Christ God was reconciling the world to himself, not counting their trespasses against them, and entrusting to us the message of reconciliation. 20 Therefore, we are ambassadors for Christ, God making his appeal through us. We implore you on behalf of Christ, be reconciled to God.*

Having been reconciled to God, we are then given this amazing opportunity to be part of His plan to reconcile others to Himself. We are permitted through grace to participate in the process whereby God makes peace with other human beings. God, who has reconciled us to Himself through Jesus Christ, has also given us the ministry of reconciliation. He has given us the message of reconciliation to preach to others. Therefore, we are ambassadors for Christ, appealing to others to be at peace with God – to accept the peace treaty that God offers. We are blessed with the opportunity, the charge, to being the message of the terms of peace from God to fallen people.

Jesus died to bring us this peace. Peace with God was ultimately won for us on the cross. Isaiah tells us in...

> *Isaiah 53:5*   *He was pierced for our transgressions, He was crushed for our iniquities – upon Him was the chastisement that brought us peace, and with His wounds we are healed.*

He brought peace between us and God, and He paid for that peace on the cross. In Ephesians chapter two we read that we were once far away from God, but Jesus has brought us near to God by His blood, because He Himself is our peace. Our very ability to approach near to God was bought for us by His blood. This peace with God did not come cheaply, but came with a very high price tag – which the Lord so kindly and compassionately paid for us.

> *Colossians 1:19-20*   *For in him all the fullness of God was pleased to dwell, 20 and through him to reconcile to himself all things, whether on earth or in heaven, making peace by the blood of his cross.*

God Himself made peace with us, and that peace was costly. The cost was the blood of Jesus Christ. The cost was the cross. Through His cross, reconciliation between God and man was made, and peace with God became real for us. The immeasurable value of this peace with God can be seen in the many Bible passages which describe the final destiny of those who do not make peace with Him.

DISCUSSION QUESTIONS:

1 – Discuss how vital it is for every human being to find peace with God.

2 – According to Isaiah 53:5 how was this peace with God made possible?

3 – Describe what happens to a person when they are given peace with God.

20 PEACE WITH OTHERS

In the Old Testament, the benefits of being God's chosen people were exclusive to the people of Israel. Even though the people of Israel often abandoned God, frequently disobeyed Him and left Him for other Gods, there was still this abiding exclusivity; making the people of Israel the chosen people of God, distinct from all other peoples. Gentiles are described in the Bible as being branches that are grafted into the family tree, as adopted children brought into the household of God. In Israel's history this chosen people status caused a wall of partition to be built up. And this wall separated the Jewish people from all other peoples. Part of what happened on the cross was the breaking down of that wall of partition, allowing gentiles to enter into the plan of reconciliation.

Ephesians 2:13-19   But now in Christ Jesus you who once were far off have been brought near by the blood of Christ. 14 For he himself is our peace, who has made us both one and has broken down in his flesh the dividing wall of hostility 15 by abolishing the law of commandments expressed in ordinances, that he might create in himself one new man in place of the two, so making peace, 16 and might reconcile us both to God in one body through the cross, thereby killing the hostility. 17 And he came and preached peace to you who were far off and peace to those who were near. 18 For through him we both have access in one Spirit to the Father. 19 So then you are no longer strangers and aliens, but you are fellow citizens with the saints and members of the household of God,

Jesus has reconciled us both, Jews and gentiles, to God as one new man, as a new kind of chosen people. And in reconciling both groups of people to God, He reconciles us to each other as well. The wall of separation, the wall of hostility is broken down. The significance of this particular reconciliation between Jew and gentile is that we who were once far off are now brought near. What are we brought near to? The Lord Himself; His favor, His promises, His blessings, His gifts of faith and repentance, etc. The favored nation status that Israel once enjoyed alone is now for all of us. And now God calls us to work on living at peace with others, both in the church and out of the church. We are to work towards peace with others in the way that we live among them, and in the way we live with each other.

What are we up against in this effort to live at peace with our fellow men? The unredeemed person lives basically at war with anyone and everyone who gets in the way of them getting what they want. The world of fallen man is one big aggressive and passive aggressive battlefield where every man and every woman, and yes, even every child, is at war with everybody else to get something or to gain some advantage. All you have to do to see the truth of this is think back and remember life with your siblings, or life in middle school, and I think you will agree that the whole world is at war with each other.

It is only the redemption of our souls through Jesus Christ that enables us to live at peace with each other. And that peace, which is a fruit of the Holy Spirit, is progressively gained as we mature in our lives with the Lord. This fruit of peace will be developed in our lives by the Holy Spirit as He does His work in us. From my experience, as far as any of the different fruits of the Spirit go, this growth is brought about by putting us into circumstances that will demonstrate where we are in that progress – so that we can see who we truly are. It is like God, through His word, holds up a mirror for you to look into, and by looking you can see the relative ugliness or beauty you have in that given area. And because our example and our standard is always the perfection of Jesus Christ, the picture in the mirror is always unflattering. And the believer who can mature more quickly is the believer who can better endure seeing their own moral ugliness and desire to be better. Often, though, the human reaction to having your moral ugliness revealed to you is to deny it; to say, "no, no, that's not me, I'm a nice person. I'm a good person. It's the other one who is the morally wrong one, not me. Never me." So then, the one who will grow more is the one who learns to agree with the picture of themselves that God shows them, and who then puts effort into changing. But, of course, it is not our own effort that brings about the change. It has always fascinated me how the Bible attributes all progress in these areas of spiritual maturation to God alone. We only grow because of God. We only mature because of His work in us. But at the same time the Bible does not stop demanding effort from us towards the goals of spiritual maturity. This apparent contradiction is just part of the Christian life. The Bible puts forth both ideas as truth. Any transformation in our character depends wholly on God doing what only God can do. And yet, effort in the direction of change is demanded of us. In all of this we are to understand that any change in us toward a more Christ-like life does not at all depend on us. And yet, we are called upon to live as though it all depended on us.

*Hebrews 12:14   Strive for peace with everyone,
and for the holiness without which no one will see
the Lord.*

Strive for peace with everyone.   Strive is a pretty muscular word.   It is not just simply giving it a half-hearted shot.   No, striving has a strenuousness to it – a great exertion.   So even though it is clearly the Lord who develops His fruit in us, we are not permitted to sit on the sideline and just watch the whole thing happen. We are to be in the trenches, giving it everything we've got. Look what Paul says about his own experience along these lines.

*I Corinthians 15:9-10   For I am the least of
the apostles, unworthy to be called an apostle,
because I persecuted the church of God. 10 But by
the grace of God I am what I am, and his grace
toward me was not in vain. On the contrary, I
worked harder than any of them, though it was
not I, but the grace of God that is with me.*

So, although Paul says that he started out far behind the other Apostles, he worked harder than all of them.   Why? Because he saw clearly his unworthiness relative to them.   And seeing this ugly condition he was in, did not cause him to turn away in self-pity. Instead, it made him work harder than all the rest, so that he could grow into the role God had for him. So our ability to grow is connected to our understanding of where we really are, which then must motivate us to cooperate with the Holy Spirit by working harder to get where we need to go. And like an understanding man of God, Paul wisely and rightly attributes even his extra hard work to the grace of God, because God even causes our effort. He says, "I worked harder than any of them, though it was not I, but the grace of God that is with me." Hebrews 12:14 tells us to strive, to make great effort to be at peace with everyone, Christian or non-Christian. And we read that Paul backs this up in...

Romans 12:18   If possible, so far as it depends on you, live peaceably with all.

As much as it depends on you, he says, live at peace with all. So we can see our personal responsibility to make the effort. If there is anything we can do to help make peace with others, we are clearly told to do so. Do whatever you can do. Do as much as depends on you.

But we can also see that sometimes all of our personal effort may not make peace happen, because it does not depend on us alone. Being at peace with others is not always possible. Between two believers, though, it should almost always be possible. Why? Because as Christians we are supposed to live no longer for ourselves, no longer seeking our own good above the good of others. But we are to be seeking the good of the other as much as or even more than our own good. And if two people are truly living like that, they will have peace.

> *Philippians 2:3-4   Do nothing from selfish ambition or conceit, but in humility count others more significant than yourselves. 4 Let each of you look not only to his own interests, but also to the interests of others*

As I said, if two people are living this way; counting the other as more significant than themselves, looking to the interests of the other and not just their own interests, then peace will automatically ensue. But as long as one is not living that way then there is a chance that peace will be out of reach.

So as far as our peace with each other as believers goes, it should almost always be possible. I want to say it should always happen between believers, but experience and history tell me that is often not the case, even though it should be. We are members of one body, the body of Jesus Christ. And one evidence of the Spirit's work in our lives is the extent to which we can live at peace with each other. To work for peace in our relationships will require that we no longer insist that others meet perfect standards of performance. To work for peace in our relationships requires that we put aside our grievances and forbear and forgive. To work for peace in our relationships demands the kind of sustained humility that Jesus Himself demonstrated.

Colossians tells us to let the peace of Christ rule in our hearts. Let the peace of God constrain you to act and to react in godly, peaceful ways. So peace between believers should be the rule, not the exception. However, there can be exceptions. For example, where major doctrinal differences exist, the ability to work together for the gospel can be hindered. I once was an associate pastor at a church back east. The lead pastor began to introduce some ideas about spiritual authority that were troubling to me. The idea was that a pastor, due to his God-given authority in the lives of his people, could actually make decisions for church members about their lives. The pastor could make decisions about their career choices, decisions about who they would marry, when they would marry, where they would live, and such things.

This was so obviously disturbing me, that the pastor felt the need to speak to me privately about it, and told me an amazing thing. Here is the thing that the pastor said; "if you disagree with me on this, I suppose that is ok. But even if you are right and I am wrong, unity is more important than the truth, so we must stick together on this issue. We must stand together, right or wrong."

This is when I made the decision to leave that church, because in my mind the truth is often more important than unity in the Bible. I suppose I could have stayed and tried to persuade others against this false teaching, but I didn't think it was possible to succeed at that. I just happened to be reading about Charles Spurgeon and the downgrade controversy at the time, which helped me to understand that doctrinal differences can and should sometimes lead to breaking of unity. How can two people walk together unless they are in agreement? At least on the major gospel issues? But between believers much more peace is possible than is often experienced. And we are clearly told to strive for peace.

Between believers and unbelievers, peace can be much more difficult. The Lord warned us that our peace with the people of the world may be impossible simply because we are connected to Him.

Matthew 10:34-38   Do not think that I have come to bring peace to the earth. I have not come to bring peace, but a sword. 35 For I

*have come to set a man against his father, and
a daughter against her mother, and a daughter-
in-law against her mother-in-law. 36 And a
person's enemies will be those of his own
household. 37 Whoever loves father or mother
more than me is not worthy of me, and whoever
loves son or daughter more than me is not worthy
of me. 38 And whoever does not take his cross
and follow me is not worthy of me.*

The gospel itself brings trouble between people.
The trouble it brings is really a trouble between
people and the Lord.   But when we are openly
associated with Jesus, when we declare that we are
His followers, then the anger that the world feels
towards the Lord finds its focus on us. And for that
reason, we should not expect to find the people of
the world being at peace with us all the time. If
we can make peace without compromise then we
should.   Because there is a promised blessing to
those who make peace.

*Matthew 5:9   Blessed are the peacemakers, for
they shall be called sons of God.*

But, of course, history is filled with conflicts
between the people of the world and the people of
God. There is often little that believers can do about
this, except to take advantage of the time we have

to be the pillar of the truth on earth (I Timothy 3:15), and face whatever backlash that entails with faithfulness and trust in God.

DISCUSSION QUESTIONS:

1 – What does it mean that Jesus has broken down the wall of separation between Jew and gentile?

2 – Why should it almost always be possible for there to be peace between any two Christians?

3 – Why is peace between Christians and the world difficult?

21 THE PEACE OF GOD

Isaiah 26:3   You keep him in perfect peace whose mind is stayed on you, because he trusts in you.

Here Isaiah gives us a beautiful picture of the peace of God, and he also gives is a clear picture of the thing in us that attaches to this peace – trust in God. The peace that comes from trusting God is described as perfect peace. The peace is so perfect that there is no worrying about things. There is no pattern of being concerned about the supply of our needs. There is no anxiety in that space of time between the realization of the need and the provision of the supply. That is the place where worry, anxiety and fear often dominate. But when you have the peace of God, there is no stress, no difficulty, no turmoil, no unrest, in that time between the realization of the need and the supply of it. What fills this space instead of the old and usual anxieties? Trust and peace.

Matthew 6:25-34   Therefore I tell you, do not be anxious about your life, what you will eat or what you will drink, nor about your body, what you will put on. Is not life more than food, and the body more than clothing? *26* Look at the birds of the air: they neither sow nor reap nor gather into barns, and yet your heavenly Father feeds them. Are you not of more value than they? *27* And which of you by being anxious can add a single hour to his span of life? *28* And why are you anxious about clothing? Consider the lilies of the field, how they grow: they neither toil nor spin, *29* yet I tell you, even Solomon in all his glory was not arrayed like one of these. *30* But if God so clothes the grass of the field, which today is alive and tomorrow is thrown into the oven, will he not much more clothe you, O you of little faith? *31* Therefore do not be anxious, saying, 'What shall we eat?' or 'What shall we drink?' or 'What shall we wear?' *32* For the Gentiles seek after all these things, and your heavenly Father knows that you need them all. *33* But seek first the kingdom of God and his righteousness, and all these things will be added to you. *34* "Therefore do not be anxious about tomorrow, for tomorrow will be anxious for itself. Sufficient for the day is its own trouble.

The peace of God removes practical worries. The needs for food, drink and clothing are here covered, taken care of by the Lord. Here we find commands and promises mixed up together into one big, beautiful stew of peace. In verse twenty-five we are commanded "do not be anxious" about our practical, physical needs. In verse twenty-six we are told to notice how God takes care of the lowlier animals and understand that He considers us to be much more important than them. If He takes such good care of them, then don't you think He will do the same for us? In verse twenty-seven we learn that our worry is not productive, and cannot accomplish anything for us. In verses twenty-eight through thirty we learn that since God clothes nature in such a beautiful way, we can be sure our needs for clothing and warmth will be met. In verse thirty-one and thirty-two we are commanded, "don't be anxious," because God knows all about our needs. Let the unbelievers seek these things in their own way, but we are to be different. In verse thirty-three is the capstone commandment in the passage; "seek first, seek foremost, seek primarily, seek mainly the kingdom of God and His righteousness, and all these other things which the world chases after – all these other things which are actually necessary for life - will simply be provided for you." And again, in verse thirty-four we are commanded, "do not be anxious."

So, what can we learn from this? The Lord seems to be comparing two kinds of seeking. And He seems to be saying that one kind of seeking is more important than the other. He is saying chase after the spiritual things rather than the practical things. Eternity is way more important than the here and now. People who come into the kingdom of God should not view the material things of earthly life as others view them. They should put God's interests first. They should put the things involving the Kingdom of God ahead of even our own practical needs.

So, there are two things we can do to help ourselves to have more of the peace of God in our lives. One, we can simply trust Him. We can trust His word; trust His promises, trust His nature and His character as the Bible reveals them, and trust His forgiveness. We can trust Him because He is faithful. Two, we can focus our seeking on seeking His things. We can focus our seeking on seeking the kingdom of God and His righteousness, and put all the physical things on the backburner. This peace which is the fruit of the Spirit is the peace of...

> *Philippians 4:6-7*   *do not be anxious about anything, but in everything by prayer and supplication with thanksgiving let your requests be made known to God. 7 And the peace of God, which surpasses all understanding, will guard your hearts and your minds in Christ Jesus.*

The usual response to troubling circumstances is to be anxious. But instead of that, we pray. We cast our cares on Him because we know that He cares for us. And somehow, this act of trust that prayer is, miraculously transfers all that anxiety and worry over to Him. Instead of being anxious, instead of being torn up and worried and distressed about the things that are happening, we take all of it, we bring it to our father, and we pray. And we make supplication. Which is coming to God in all humility. Which is coming to God with the understanding that although there is nothing we can do about our troubles, there is nothing He cannot do about our troubles, because nothing is impossible for God. And this simple act of trust, which is what prayer is, miraculously transfers all that worry and anxiety over to Him. And then, the peace of God that transcends our own understanding will guard our hearts and minds.

This peace surpasses all understanding. When others see you in a state of peace despite the things they know are going on in your life, they can't make sense of it. It surpasses their understanding. It does not make sense according to what can be seen in your life as many things that ought to cause you distress are obviously not doing so. The peace you have seems out of place. And the promise is that once we have put the matter into God's hands through prayer, then we can relax and let the peace of God cover us. As we trust Him and put things into His problem box, they are no longer in our problem box, so we can relax, knowing He has got this.

DISCUSSION QUESTIONS:

1 – Does the knowledge that God is your Father and will see to your needs make it easier for you to seek His things ahead of your own things?

2 – Can you point to a situation, a time and place in your life, when the peace that you experienced didn't match up with the turmoil in the circumstance?

3 – Do you have a peace about your salvation? Be honest. Discuss it and pray with others.

22 PATIENCE DESCRIBED

Galatians 5:22-25   But the fruit of the Spirit is love, joy, peace, patience, kindness, goodness, faithfulness, 23 gentleness, self-control; against such things there is no law. 24 And those who belong to Christ Jesus have crucified the flesh with its passions and desires. 25 If we live by the Spirit, let us also keep in step with the Spirit.

The fruit of the Spirit is patience. As we have been studying the fruit of the Spirit, I have come to appreciate that these different aspects of the fruit of the Spirit can be seen as coming together to give us a better picture of the character of God. The fruit of the Spirit only comes into our lives through the work of the Holy Spirit. It all emanates from God Himself. So, when we say that the fruit of the Spirit is patience, it is the same thing as saying that God is patient, or, God is patience. So that all of these different fruits of the Spirit come together and give us a picture of our great God. He is loving, joyful, peaceful, patient, kind, good, faithful, gentle and self-controlled.

The word for patience is translated as longsuffering in many translations. I like that word for patience – longsuffering. It seems to fit so well when thinking of God's patience towards us. He suffers long for us. He bears with a lot of stuff from us for a very long time without bringing judgement. He is rich in mercy and slow to anger. He suffers from our rebellion for a very long time. He endures our indifference for a very long time. He tolerates our affront to His holy character for a very long time. He endures a lot of junk from us without bringing immediate judgement. And all the while, as He is waiting, He remains faithful to us, whether we are behaving with faithfulness toward Him or not. It isn't even just that He waits. It isn't just that He withholds judgement for such a long time, but it is also how He waits. He waits for us with loving intentions. He waits with a good plan in mind for us. He waits faithfully during our unfaithfulness. All the while preparing a place for us to be with him.

Patience means long-tempered. Which is the opposite of short-tempered. We all probably know what it is like to be around short-tempered people. So, what a relief then to know that God is long-tempered. One who is long-tempered takes a longer time to come to an angry boil. They don't reach that intense, impassioned response to things quickly. God is patient. God is patience.

And, of course, these aspects of the fruit of the Spirit are things which our God desires to see in us. He means for us to bear this fruit. He teaches us patience in his word. He teaches us patience through the experiences He leads us through. He teaches us patience not just by making a rule, not just by commanding us to be patient, but He also provides us an example in the Lord Himelf. But He even goes beyond simply providing an example. He doesn't just say "Jesus is patient, so you be patient." He even goes so much further than that to teach us. He teaches us patience by being patient with us. This is profound to me, because now, each one of us who know Him have first-hand experience with the patience of God. We know personally what it is like for someone to have patience with us. And the same is true for all the other parts of the fruit of the Spirit. We know what it is to be loved by God, to have His joy and His peace imparted to us. We know His patience, His kindness, His goodness and His gentleness. We know His faithfulness.

Up until now we have looked at love, joy and peace. Those are things that we all ordinarily want to have in our own arsenal of attitudes. They are things we could easily enough picture ourselves pursuing. They are things that any reasonable person would chase after. Who doesn't want love joy and peace? I want to be a person who loves others. I want to be a person who experiences joy and peace. I want gladness and rest, happiness and calm. But patience is different. It is difficult to imagine someone setting out on a quest for patience. It is not normal to try and become more patient. Now, we certainly would like for others to be more patient with us. And in life we sometimes ask others to be more patient with us. But to say to yourself, "I want to become a more patient person," is not a normal human thing. Patience is not a thing we naturally strive for. Why don't people ordinarily try to become more patient? Because, built into patience is the understanding that it is only needed because something is wrong. Why do you need patience? Because something is not right. Because something is not good. Something is not the way you want it to be. Something good that you want is being delayed or withheld from you. Something bad is lingering in your life for way too long. Somebody is getting on your last nerve. Something in your life is persistently painful or uncomfortable. There is some kind of pressure that you want to get out from under. So, we just know that if we are being called upon to be patient, that means something is not going to be good. And probably it will be that way for a lot longer than we are comfortable with.

Patience isn't just waiting for something. It is not just waiting for something to finally begin or to finally end. Patience is how you deal with things that are wrong and unpleasant over the long haul. Patience is how you respond to seemingly immoveable problems which do not have a clear-cut end point. Patience is what you do while you wait. Patience is the attitude in which you wait. We know that normal Christian life requires the development of patience because the normal Christian life is full of troubles. Listen to what Paul tells some of the believers on one of his journeys.

> *Acts 14:21-22   When they had preached the gospel to that city and had made many disciples, they returned to Lystra and to Iconium and to Antioch, 22 strengthening the souls of the disciples, encouraging them to continue in the faith, and saying that through many tribulations we must enter the kingdom of God.*

Through many tribulations we must enter the kingdom of God. A side note here; just prior to returning to the cities of Iconium and Antioch, Paul had been stoned by the people of those cities. They thought they had killed him, but he miraculously survived. So then, these believers knew what Paul had been through, they had seen it themselves. They were first-hand witnesses to some of the things that believers must get through. Paul now comes back to see them. He is trying to strengthen them and encourage them to continue in the faith. Christians can sometimes come into a danger of giving up. A danger of not continuing in the faith.

So then, they (and we) need to be strengthened sometimes. We need encouragement to continue in the faith now and then. Why? Because it is hard. And with what encouraging words does Paul strengthen them? He tells them that through many tribulations we must enter the kingdom of God. And because that is true, for them at that time, and for us now, becoming people who bear the fruit of patience is very vital for us. Patience is needed in order for us to be people who continue in the faith.

DISCUSSION QUESTIONS:

1 – Does understanding God's patient, long-suffering attitude toward you help you to respond in like manner to others?

2 – Where do you have the most difficulty being patient? At home? At work? At school? Why?

3 – Why is it important for Christians to be patient people?

23 THE PATIENCE OF GOD

Exodus 34:6   The Lord passed before him and proclaimed, "The Lord, the Lord, a God merciful and gracious, slow to anger, and abounding in steadfast love and faithfulness,"

An interesting and significant thing about this verse is that the events depicted in it happened because of a prayer, a request from Moses. In Exodus 33:18 Moses said to God, "Please show me your glory." And God replied, "I will make all my goodness pass before you and will proclaim before you my name "The Lord." As the Lord agrees to show Moses His glory, there is a visual aspect to the act of showing Moses who He is, and there is also an auditory aspect of showing Moses His glory. "The Lord, the Lord, a God merciful and gracious, slow to anger, and abounding in steadfast love and faithfulness," is heard as God passes by. Part of His glory is that He is merciful, gracious, slow to anger and abounding in steadfast love and faithfulness. God is slow to anger. He is longsuffering, long-tempered, patient. God is patience, but God's patience can be misunderstood.

> II Peter 3:4   They will say, "Where is the promise of his coming? For ever since the fathers fell asleep, all things are continuing as they were from the beginning of creation."

Peter says that scoffers in the last days will mistake God's patience for disinterest, indifference or inability. "Where is He?" they will ask. "He promised to come back but has not come." But a few verses later Peter tells us why the Lord delays.

> II Peter 3:9   The Lord is not slow to fulfill his promise as some count slowness, but is patient toward you, not wishing that any should perish, but that all should reach repentance.

It is not that God is slow to fulfill His promises. It is not that He has forgotten to come back and judge. It is not that He has become indifferent to sin. He is patient for the number of those to be saved to fill all the way up to its appointed number. He delays His return so that additional offers of grace can be made and heard and responded to. The Lord is not slow to fulfill His promise. In other words, people should not conclude that because His promise seems delayed that it is late in coming because His promise will fail. When people go a long time without fulfilling their promises to us, we begin to think they didn't mean it when they promised, or maybe they changed their mind, or maybe they forgot. But it would be foolish and faithless to make those same kinds of assumptions when God's promise seems delayed. For whatever reason, if a promise of God seems to be deferred in your life, if it seems to be delayed, you can be certain it is not for any carelessness, or forgetfulness, or change of mind, or failure of character in God.

Peter says that the Lord is not slow to fulfill his promise as some count slowness. There may have been some impatient Christians of his day expressing these kinds of concerns about the Lord's seeming delay. But Peter assures them and us that God's apparent delay should be considered as proof of His patience, proof of His longsuffering attitude toward us. He does not wish that any should perish, but that all should reach repentance. His patience is merciful and purposeful.

Paul also describes the great patience of God. Paul says that he received mercy just so that God could demonstrate His patience for others to see.

I Timothy 1:15-16   The saying is trustworthy

*and deserving of full acceptance, that Christ
Jesus came into the world to save sinners, of whom
I am the foremost. 16 But I received mercy for this
reason, that in me, as the foremost, Jesus Christ
might display his perfect patience as an example
to those who were to believe in him for eternal life.*

Paul is saying that since the Lord had patience
with him, as the absolute worst of sinners, then
He is even more likely to have mercy on and to
have patience with you lesser sinners. "Look how
patient God is!!" says Paul. "He had mercy even on
me, the guy who persecuted the church." Paul said
that his salvation was a deliberate display of the
patience of God for others to see.

God is patient. His patience is part of His
glory that He showed to Moses, and that He shows
to us on a regular basis in our own lives. He is
slow to anger, slow to bring judgement because
He does not wish that any should perish. He
may even demonstrate His great patience to others
by displaying His patient mercy to us, as He did
through Paul. Are we all convinced that God is
patient?

DISCUSSION QUESTIONS:

1 – Why does God sometime seem to delay His
judgement?

2 – How is Paul's salvation a picture of God's patience?

3 – Describe a way in which you hope be a more patient person.

24 THE IMPATIENCE
OF MAN

Numbers 20:2-12   Now there was no water for the congregation. And they assembled themselves together against Moses and against Aaron. 3 And the people quarreled with Moses and said, "Would that we had perished when our brothers perished before the Lord! 4 Why have you brought the assembly of the Lord into this wilderness, that we should die here, both we and our cattle? 5 And why have you made us come up out of Egypt to bring us to this evil place? It is no place for grain or figs or vines or pomegranates, and there is no water to drink." 6 Then Moses and Aaron went from the presence of the assembly to the entrance of the tent of meeting and fell on their faces. And the glory of the Lord appeared to them, 7 and the Lord spoke to Moses, saying, 8 "Take the staff, and assemble the congregation, you and Aaron your brother, and tell the rock before their eyes to yield its water. So you shall bring water out of the rock for them and give drink to the congregation and their cattle." 9 And Moses took the staff from before the Lord, as he commanded him. 10 Then Moses and Aaron gathered the assembly together before the rock, and he said to them, "Hear now, you rebels: shall we bring water for you out of this rock?" 11 And Moses lifted up his hand and struck the rock with his staff twice, and water came out abundantly, and the congregation drank, and their livestock. 12 And the Lord said to Moses and Aaron, "Because you did not believe in me, to uphold me as holy in the eyes of the people of Israel, therefore you shall not bring this assembly into the land that I have given them."

This is a story of double human impatience. The people are impatient for God's provision, and Moses and Aaron are impatient over the people's impatience.

Something to understand about the appearance of impatience is this, it is often based on a real problem. In verse two there was no water for the congregation. I don't know if any of us have ever faced such a dire condition in the testing of our faith. They had no water. The problem was real and immediate and serious. There may be a lot of things that you and I want but do not have today. But I would guess that if we don't get them by next week, we will still be alive. Maybe not so for them. The people needed water, and the need was life threatening. The problems we human beings face which stir up the feelings of impatience are often not fake problems. There can be a real desperate lack of something that is needed. There can be the presence of some actual trouble that is sincerely life-threatening, like a serious disease. So impatience can often come about through the experiences of reality. Like when the disciples were in the storm at sea in the boat while Jesus slept. The storm was real, the sense of danger was real. They were certain that they would soon be killed. The storm was raging, the Lord was sleeping, so they woke Him up saying, "Teacher, don't you care that we are perishing?" It's a curious thing to ask God. "Don't you care?" Their impatience made them question God's character, it made them wonder about His true intentions toward them. Just like the Israelites in the wilderness when there was no water. The situation stirred them up to quarrel with Moses and Aaron. They gathered together to accuse the leaders of misleading them. "This is so bad," they said, "that it would have been better for us if we had died with our brothers earlier on this trip. Why did you bring us and our animals and our families out here where there is no water? And why did you lead us out of Egypt in the first place? Nothing will ever grow out here! How will we farm? How will we survive?" The people of Israel accused Moses and Aaron of misleading them, and indirectly accused God of the same thing.

This experience is very upsetting to Moses and Aaron too. They fall on their faces before the Lord. God, as He always does, faithfully speaks to them. He says...

> *Numbers 20:8   "Take the staff, and assemble the congregation, you and Aaron your brother, and tell the rock before their eyes to yield its water. So you shall bring water out of the rock for them and give drink to the congregation and their cattle."*

"Go Moses and Aaron," the Lord says, "gather the people together and speak to the rock. Tell the rock to yield its water. Just talk and water will come out of the rock, enough to meet all of their needs." How patient God is in this moment. But Moses had now grown very impatient himself. He was upset with the people because they were slow to come around and have faith in God. They were too slow to mature in Moses' eyes, I suppose. So here is what Moses did. He took the staff as God had commanded him. So far so good. But then he says, "listen to me, all of you rebels!" Moses is angry, very angry. He says "do me and Aaron have to bring water for you rebellious people out of this rock?" Then he strikes the rock twice with his staff, and the water comes out. Out of anger, out of impatience with the people, Moses yelled at them and struck the rock instead of obeying God and just speaking to the rock. The people were impatient with Moses and Aaron, and with the Lord, for not meeting their needs in a timely manner. This made Moses get impatient with the people for their lack of faith. He called them rebels. He saw them as rebelling against God by rebelling against him. But the Lord God took what Moses did as the greater rebellion. At least what Moses did was given the greater punishment by God. Because of this one moment, because of this single flash of indignant impatience toward the people of God, Moses and Aaron are not permitted to enter the land of promise. The people were not punished, but the leaders were. The call to be patient is more consequential for leaders than for others.

These two examples of the impatience of man in one story may reveal some types of impatience that could be found in us. Impatience with God for His provision, and impatience with the spiritual growth or progress in other people. There are various ways that we could probably describe all the different kinds of impatience we can be guilty of, but I would like to keep it simple.

DISCUSSION QUESTIONS:

1 – Have you been impatient with the spiritual progress of others?

2 – Why did the impatience of Moses draw a greater response from God than the impatience of the people of Israel did?

3 – Does the understanding of God's great patience and His goodness lead you to reconsider being impatient with His provision in your life?

25 TWO TYPES OF PATIENCE NEEDED

I would like for us to try and understand a couple of different ways that the Lord asks us to have patience. I think we can group almost all patience under two headings. These types of patience, these situations that call for patience are seen repeatedly in the Bible. In what ways does God call on us to be patient? He asks for a kind of steadfastness in enduring trials, and He asks for a slowness in avenging wrongs that are done to us. The Lord asks us to endure our troubles with faith and patience, knowing that in the end He will sort all things out in a perfect way, and He asks for a firm resistance in us to seeking our own vengeance, since vengeance and all true justice belong to Him.

1 STEADFASTNESS IN ENDURING TRIALS

There are many kinds of trials that Christians

are called upon to go throuh. But there is a general pattern that many of them follow. There is a problem that arises, and in that problem there is a temptation to find our own way out of the problem. There is a strong desire to get out from the pain of the circumstance. But since the problem comes with God's purpose in it, to accomplish His work in us, we must exercise patience in dealing with it. We must lerarn to endure through the trouble so that it can do what it came to accomplish.

> *James 1:2-4   Count it all joy, my brothers, when you meet trials of various kinds, 3 for you know that the testing of your faith produces steadfastness. 4 And let steadfastness have its full effect, that you may be perfect and complete, lacking in nothing.*

Count it all joy when you go through various trials. This joy comes through the knowledge that trials help believers to develop steadfastness, which is endurance, which is patience - and this strengthens Christian character. So we can know with certainty that any trial which our God permits to come into our lives is sent to further develop our Christian character as the fruit of His Spirit. One hundred percent of the trials that a Christian goes through, if endured in the right frame of mind and heart, will result in the personal growth of the believer, either in patience or one of the other aspects of the fruit of the Spirit. That is the purpose of God in the trials of His beloved children, and nothing and nobody can thwart His purposes.

Now the testing of your faith is never really for God's benefit. God knows the truth about you the whole time. The testing of your faith is not so that the Lord can discern where you stand or how well you will do in the test. Instead, the test is for you to get a clearer picture of where you stand. Some may think that if they fail some test then God has discovered some new flaw in them which He didn't previously know about. You may disappoint or surprise yourself, but it is not even possible to disappoint or surprise God. God knows precisely what we are made of and He never discovers something new in us. So God cannot really be disappointed in us in the same way we can disappoint each other or even ourselves. We disappoint ourselves because we often think we are further down the road than we really are. "I thought I was over that hump. I thought I had conquered that area. And here comes the situation where I'm tested and man, I blow it. I'm so disappointed. Why did I say that? Why did I do that?" But I shouldn't feel condemned like "Oh, I've let God down," or "I disappointed God." No, because God knew it the whole time. But I needed to know it. And so, God allowed the situation so I could find it out.

Count it all joy because this testing of our faith develops patience, or works patience. What a much-needed quality patience is. So often our failure is in waiting upon God. And that is true throughout the Bible. So many people within the Scriptures got into trouble because they didn't wait upon God. They failed in the test of faith in various areas of their lives. Abraham passed the test magnificently with Isaac, when the Lord asked him to give his son back to God. Yet he utterly failed in the birth of Isaac. When God promised to give him a son. He wasn't patient. Sarah came to him and said something like, "oh, come on, Abraham; it's not going to work. You take my handmaid and you have a son by her. And when the child is born it will be as my child. It just doesn't seem like I can even have a baby, Abraham!"

Abraham and Sarah failed in their faith. They didn't wait for God to do what He had promised them He would do. They became anxious, impatient, unable to wait. They implemented their own plan to bring about the promise of God. The testing of our faith develops patience. But, like Abraham, whenever we do not wait upon God, we are messing things up, creating new and unnecessary problems for ourselves. And so, it's important that we're tested. It is crucial that we learn to wait upon God, knowing this, that the trying of our faith works patience. But let steadfastness have its full effect, so that we might be fully matured. And that's the whole purpose of God is to bring us into a maturity, where we will no longer respond like little children to the disappointments of life. But that we grow up and become mature and complete, lacking nothing.

2 SLOWNESS IN AVENGING WRONGS DONE TO US

> *Matthew 18:21-22   Then Peter came up and said to him, "Lord, how often will my brother sin against me, and I forgive him? As many as seven times?" 22 Jesus said to him, "I do not say to you seven times, but seventy-seven times.*

At what point in being offended and hurt by someone am I allowed to stop forgiving and seek my vengeance? How much do I have to put up with before I am finally allowed to hit back? If you have a desire to get even, if you are hoping for your chance to make things humanly right, then these numbers might be discouraging to you. The Lord tells Peter to forgive his brother who offends him seventy-seven times. In the book of Amos, the prophet goes through a series of descriptions of the transgressions of various nations, and for each of them it seems like the first three times they have sinned it is forgiven. At the fourth transgression, judgement comes and no more forgiveness is needed. So maybe Peter was thinking of this, and so by offering to forgive the offender seven times, he was thinking that he was going far above and beyond what God requires for forgiving wrongs done to us. Seven is a lot more than just three. But the Lord took him and us to a whole new level of forgiving and not seeking to repay. The Lord would like for us to be slow in avenging wrongs. In fact, let me show you something. Have you ever wanted to know what God has called you to do in life? I can show you one thing that you are called to do right now.

> *I Peter 2:20-21   For what credit is it if, when you sin and are beaten for it, you endure? But if when you do good and suffer for it you endure, this is a gracious thing in the sight of God. 21 For to this you have been called, because Christ also suffered for you, leaving you an example, so that you might follow in his steps.*

What has God called me to do? What does it mean to follow Jesus Christ? Here it is; I am called to suffer for doing the right thing. Peter says this, "endure it gracefully when you are treated unfairly." Then he says, "to this you are called." One of the things then, that we are called to do as Christians is to suffer gracefully when we are treated unfairly. Endure it without seeking revenge or redress. When you see someone behave in this way, then you know that you are seeing a mature Christian.

DISCUSSION QUESTIONS:

1 – What does it mean to be steadfast in enduring trials?

2 – What does it mean to be slow in avenging wrongs?

3 – Which of these two types of patience above presents the greatest challenge to you?

26 WHY WE NEED PATIENCE

1 BECAUSE GOD IS PATIENT WITH US

> *Colossians 3:12-13   Put on then, as God's chosen ones, holy and beloved, compassionate hearts, kindness, humility, meekness, and patience, 13 bearing with one another and, if one has a complaint against another, forgiving each other; as the Lord has forgiven you, so you also must forgive.*

The aspect of patience that involves being slow to avenge wrongs is so closely connected to forgiveness, that they are nearly indistinguishable from a human perspective. Being slow to seek vengeance is giving room for potential repentance. And when we consider the immenseness of the debt of forgiveness and patience which we owe to God, we are compelled to forgive and be patient with others. We ought to at least be largely inclined to give ample room for repentance.

It is when we put on such things as Paul lists, like compassionate hearts, kindness, humility, meekness and patience; that we begin to have the family resemblance to Jesus Himself. It is then that we actually look like God's chosen, elect ones. It is then that it is not us who are living, but it is Jesus Christ who is living in us.

2   IN ORDER TO MAINTAIN UNITY IN FELLOWSHIP

> *Ephesians 4:1-3   I therefore, a prisoner for the Lord, urge you to walk in a manner worthy of the calling to which you have been called, 2 with all humility and gentleness, with patience, bearing with one another in love, 3 eager to maintain the unity of the Spirit in the bond of peace.*

Without patience, the sins we commit against one another will quickly destroy the unity for which Christ died! In this passage, patience is grouped together with humility and gentleness. This is an appropriate grouping. Often patience and humility are needed together. Otherwise, the foolish flesh may begin to proudly argue that it somehow deserves to be treated in some higher way than it is experiencing. It is much easier to lose patience with someone who you feel superior to. But when you rightly view yourself from the humble aspect of reality, you are more ready to be patient with people who are either wronging you or are not maturing as fast as you would like them to. Patience paired with gentleness is also spot on. Impatience can be so ungentle and rough. Remembering who we once were and how gentle and patient the Lord has been with us ought to remind us of the need for patience to be evident in our attitudes toward others.

3 PATIENCE NEEDED FOR ALL LEADERS AND DISCIPLERS

> *II Timothy 4:2   preach the word; be ready in season and out of season; reprove, rebuke, and exhort, with complete patience and teaching.*

Anyone who would lead another needs patience. All reproving, rebuking and exhorting needs to be done with complete patience. Otherwise, the reproving and rebuking devolves into a kind of cynical criticism. To reprove here means to censure, to express disapproval over some behavior. To rebuke is very similar, only stronger and more authoritative. To exhort is to make a strong, persuasive appeal or argument for change.

All of these require an attitude of patience in the leader.

DISCUSSION QUESTIONS:

1 – Does the recognition that God has been very patient with you have an impact on how patient you ought to be toward others?

2 – Describe how impatience could do damage to the unity of fellowship among believers.

3 – Why does a Christian leader need to be patient?

27 HOW PATIENCE IS DEVELOPED IN US

1 THROUGH LOVE

> *I Corinthians 13:4-7   Love is patient and kind; love does not envy or boast; it is not arrogant 5 or rude. It does not insist on its own way; it is not irritable or resentful; 6 it does not rejoice at wrongdoing, but rejoices with the truth. 7 Love bears all things, believes all things, hopes all things, endures all things.*

In I Corinthians 13 we learn that love is patient. It is love which suffers long and keeps showing kindness without becoming rude or arrogant. Unless we love those who have wronged us, there will not be sufficient motivation to bear with them in patience. Therefore love (active good will) is fundamental to being slow to avenge wrong. By growing in love, we will grow in patience!

2 THROUGH PRAYER

> *Colossians 1:9-11   And so, from the day we heard, we have not ceased to pray for you, asking that you may be filled with the knowledge of his will in all spiritual wisdom and understanding, 10 so as to walk in a manner worthy of the Lord, fully pleasing to him: bearing fruit in every good work and increasing in the knowledge of God; 11 being strengthened with all power, according to his glorious might, for all endurance and patience with joy;*

Part of Paul's prayer for the Colossians is that they would have more endurance and patience, with joy. Paul clearly believed that prayer would help the Colossians to have **"all endurance and patience."** Otherwise, he would not have prayed for these things for his friends. Certainly, the God who is patient will strengthen those who desire and request to be like Him! So I think that we can be certain that prayers for patience will indeed be answered.

3 THROUGH SUFFERING

> *James 1:2-4   Count it all joy, my brothers,*

when you meet trials of various kinds, 3 for you know that the testing of your faith produces steadfastness. 4 And let steadfastness have its full effect, that you may be perfect and complete, lacking in nothing.

James opens his letter with these words; "Count it all joy, my brothers, when you meet trials of various kinds, for you know that the testing of your faith produces steadfastness." The word translated as "steadfastness" in the ESV could also be translated "patience," as it is in the KJV. So, according to James, it is actually life's difficulties, which come to test or to prove our faith, that ultimately work to produce patience in us. And he goes on to say that this trial-by-fire way of learning patience will leave us in a perfect and complete condition, lacking nothing. I take this to mean that this is the best way to learn patience, in that it leaves you with a more perfect and complete kind of patience. It is often the hard learned lesson that is the best learned lesson.

DISCUSSION QUESTIONS:

1 – Describe how love can cause us to be more patient.

2 – Do you have the courage to pray for patience?

3 – Can suffering really bring about an increase in your patience? Why?

28 KINDNESS DESCRIBED

THE FRUIT OF THE SPIRIT IS KINDNESS

Galatians 5:22-25   But the fruit of the Spirit is love, joy, peace, patience, kindness, goodness, faithfulness, 23 gentleness, self-control; against such things there is no law. 24 And those who belong to Christ Jesus have crucified the flesh with its passions and desires. 25 If we live by the Spirit, let us also keep in step with the Spirit.

I don't know whether or not you have noticed, but we do not live in an especially kind world. We do not live in a world of sweet words and soft hearts. In fact, we live in a time when acting with cruelty is rather easy to do publicly. The internet with such places as twitter make it very easy to be cruel without having to actually be face to face with your victims. There is a kind of layer between you and the other people on the platform, which allows for direct communication and a kind of anonymity at the same time. With unhindered freedom to say whatever you want to say, people struggle to be kind on such platforms, even Christian people. I cannot tell you how much "Christian" cruelty I have seen on the internet. Kindness is sorely lacking in our world. I have seen theological debates turn into very unkind things on Facebook and Twitter.

And it is not just on social media where kindness is very lacking. If you have never yet spent any time in non-western third world places, I think you might be shocked at how people openly treat each other. In places where Christianity has not had quite so much social influence, people do not have the same social niceties that we are accustomed to seeing in the developed west. In many Asian cultures, for example, you will not find the general sensitivity to the suffering of the helpless, like widows and orphans. Here, in the Christian-influenced west, we have governmental and religious infrastructure which sets up care for the helpless. But there are places in the world where that is just not the case. we only have such social care for the helpless here because of centuries of Christianity's influence. The people of the western world owe much and most of the cultural kindness and care for the helpless that we experience to the influence of Christianity. Millions in Pakistan, India, China and other places live in abject squalor, with little to no hope of ever rising up the social ladder to a place of less suffering. Being born as an ethnic Christian in places like Pakistan is tantamount to a life sentence of poverty, disease and persecution. Man's default setting is selfishness and cruelty toward the weak and helpless. In the "civilized" world we are less aware of this truth because of the long-term positive impact of having the church in our midst. Where the church has not had much social influence, there is not much structural concern or care for the helpless.

We talked about patience last time, and often patience might be manifested by doing nothing. In contrast to this, kindness is demonstrated by doing something. Kindness is shown in what we say and in what we do. On a deeper level, kindness also involves how we say things and how we do things. Kindness also involves why we say things and why we do things. From God's view of things, how and why we do what we do is always significant.

We struggle to be kind on various internet platforms. And we often struggle to be kind even at home if we are willing to be honest. How many times has your first instinct been to be cruel, rather than kind, to your own family members? How often do the unkind words escape from your mouth before you seem to be able to stop them? Words that are meant to hurt, to belittle, to jab, stab, disparage and deride. This sin filled world is cursed with widespread cruelty of words and actions. Our hearts in their natural state are bent toward unkindness and selfishness. The fruit of the Spirit which is kindness does not naturally occur in human hearts. It has to be supernaturally implanted there and brought to life by God the Spirit.

I have read that the word for kindness in Galatians 5:22 might have been translated as useful. There is a practical component of being useful in the lives of others in acts of kindness. Isn't that interesting? It represents a gentle, caring disposition which we should have towards meeting the needs of others. As God shows us the needs in the lives of others, the fruit of kindness moves us to want to meet those revealed needs. The fruit of kindness in us makes us useful in meeting the need of others. So, a person who is kind is a person who can be useful or practical at meeting the needs of people whom they see in need.

Kindness is a type of active love. It is a love that does something. It is a love that does something toward the blessing of others in some way. Kindness is the medium through which the love of God becomes tangible through us. Kindness is acting in a beneficial, helpful, useful, loving way towards others. Kindness has an internal component, but also needs an outward component in order to be the real thing.

Psalm 145:17   The Lord is righteous in all his ways and kind in all his works.

In God's kindness, His ways match His works. The inner aspect matches the outer aspect. There are two aspects of kindness; an inner disposition, and an outward demonstration. The Lord is righteous in all His ways and kind in all His works. So, then the inner disposition of kindness includes having goodwill and benevolence towards others. The inner disposition delights in contributing to the happiness of others, which is done cheerfully and gladly, to meet their wishes, supply their needs or alleviate their distresses. Kindness always accompanies love. Kindness also always shows up as an outward demonstration. An act of good will; any act of benevolence which promotes the happiness or welfare of others is a kindness. Attention to the needs & desires of others are known as acts of kindness.

So here is a definition of kindness for us - Kindness is an inner disposition which delights in cheerfully advancing the happiness of others and in meeting their needs, fulfilling their wishes, and removing their distresses. It is also an outward demonstration in real actions toward the end of benefitting another.

What an amazing definition! Let's apply it to God. What do you really believe about God the Father? What is the inner disposition of God toward us? What do you believe most accurately describes God's internal motives? Is God benevolent? Or is He malevolent? I ask these things just for the purpose of getting at the heart of what we really, truly believe about God. A.W. Tozer said that the most important thing about you and me is what we think about God. Does God possess an inner disposition which delights in advancing the happiness and welfare of others? Or is He the kind of person who delights in diminishing the happiness of others? Does He cheerfully satisfy the desires of His children? Or does He begrudgingly fulfill our needs? Does our God take pleasure in answering the prayers of His children? Or is He mostly annoyed with our continual, unrelenting requests for stuff? Is God internally pleased with our ceaseless praying to Him? Or in the back of His mind, does He secretly think we talk too much? Does it make God happy to give some relief to His children who are distressed? Or does He enjoy it more to see us lay in the bed we have made for ourselves? Do you believe that God, in His essential nature, at the very core of who He is, is kind? I am speaking in a shocking way about what people can believe about God, so that we can sort of wake up to the realization that we are in good hands. The fruit of the Spirit is kindness, because the inner disposition of God is kindness. The all-powerful, all-knowing, all-seeing God of the Bible is kind. It is that simple. He is very kind. Imagine this, our God has all the power that ever was or ever will be in His very hands, and He can use this power over us in any way that He chooses. And we discover in the Bible that He is rich in loving kindness. We discover that He is for us and not against us. We discover that He is gentle and compassionate and kind toward us. We hit the jackpot! We won the grand prize!! We are the most blessed forever! Because imagine one of us, as we are in our fallen nature, having that kind of power over the lives of others? How would we treat those who got themselves into troubles and had nobody but themselves to blame? Would we be generally patient and kind with them? We are eternally blessed that God is not like us.

By contrast, the kindnesses we often see in the world today are sort of half-hearted expressions of good will or good hopes. But the kindness that is the fruit of the Spirit is tangible, touchable, real-life action on the full behalf of others.

Proverbs 12:10   Whoever is righteous has regard for the life of his beast, but the mercy of the wicked is cruel.

Our human kindness, that is not a fruit of the Spirit, will always be tainted. It will always be something that is not truly kind. It will be tainted by selfishness, self-love or even the fear of man. Maybe we will do an act of apparent kindness so that others will see and will therefore praise us. Maybe we will do an act of kindness so that others will not doubt our Christian bona fides, and they will be somehow impressed with us. Maybe it is the fear of what others may think of us that moves us towards acts of kindness. Without a connection to the True Vine, we can only show false kindness. What is false kindness? False kindness is being useful to others only when it is useful to me. False kindness has contingencies. False kindness has strings attached. It will appear at advantageous times, such as when we are being observed, or around those we like, or to get what we want. False kindness is like hashtag support; just for show but without real action. False kindness is Judas Iscariot pretending to have concern for the poor while stealing from the money bag to enrich himself.

But true kindness is generous. It flows freely and impartially to those we disagree with, those we hardly know, and those who cannot thank us or repay us. Or to those who simply WILL not thank us or repay us. True, kindness looks odd to the world. It means meeting the needs of others, without the need for recognition. It means self-sacrifice, without the thought of self-preservation. True kindness is the good Samaritan, who reached into his own pocket to meet the needs of a suffering enemy stranger. In God's true kindness, He meets the needs of His creation and He even provides for those who hate Him. He causes the rain to fall on the just and on the unjust, He causes His sun to shine even on the ungrateful. But God's kindness extends to His covenant people in a particularly special way.

> *Titus 3:4-7   But when the goodness and loving kindness of God our Savior appeared, 5 he saved us, not because of works done by us in righteousness, but according to his own mercy, by the washing of regeneration and renewal of the Holy Spirit, 6 whom he poured out on us richly through Jesus Christ our Savior, 7 so that being justified by his grace we might become heirs according to the hope of eternal life.*

We did not need to be kind people for Him to save us. God knows exactly what type of unkind people we were and yet He still met our needs in Christ. Our Savior's kindness is not lukewarm, it is not selfish, it is not there just to make Him look good to others. This is demonstrated clearly in the moments of His greatest suffering. Jesus, while on the cross, while bearing the punishment for man's sin made arrangements for the care of

His mother after He would be gone. He prayed for the forgiveness of the men who were killing Him. He spoke kind words of comfort to the thief dying beside Him. The Lord demonstrates kindness to all, but He reserves an even more special kindness for those who are His own sheep.

Ephesians 4:32 admonishes Christians to, "be kind to one another, tenderhearted, forgiving one another, as God in Christ forgave you." We reflect the character of God by abiding in Him and obeying His commands. In this amazing union between Him and us, which He causes to happen, the fruit of kindness will grow and the dispositions of our heart will be turned towards meeting the needs of others. The call to kindness is a call to action. Not only does it require the transformation of our hearts, but our desires for goodwill towards man must translate into real efforts to fill the needs of those around us and to be useful towards our brothers and sisters.

DISCUSSION QUESTIONS:

1 – Describe how kindness is love in action.

2 – Describe how a kind person could be considered to be a useful person.

3 – Discuss Proverbs 12:10

29 THE KINDNESS
OF GOD

Nehemiah 9:16-17   "But they and our fathers acted presumptuously and stiffened their neck and did not obey your commandments. 17 They refused to obey and were not mindful of the wonders that you performed among them, but they stiffened their neck and appointed a leader to return to their slavery in Egypt. But you are a God ready to forgive, gracious and merciful, slow to anger and abounding in steadfast love, and did not forsake them.

Here is the great kindness of God in a nut shell. See how the people behaved; they acted presumptuously, they stiffened their neck in mule-like stubbornness, and they refused to obey. They didn't just disobey, they refused to obey. It's like they threw an extra layer of arrogance and willfulness into the mix. They didn't even consider in their minds all the amazing miracles and wonders that God had performed on their behalf. He altered the laws of nature for them. He plagued Egypt in shocking and powerful ways. He rescued them from slavery. He saved them from certain doom at the Red Sea. He repeatedly rescued them from their own bad attitudes. And what did they do? They chose their own leader and made plans to go back into slavery. And all the while what is God doing? He is being gracious, merciful, slow to anger. He is abounding in steadfast love. He is not forsaking them, even though they are being very forsakable. Have you and I been really very forsakable people at times? Yes indeed. Did He forsake us? NO!

Kindness is doing good to those who ought to rightly expect that you will do them harm. Kindness is part love, part mercy, part compassion, and part pity. The only thing these people could possibly have rightly expected from God was anger and wrath. The same is true for all of us. And yet, what epic and beautiful kindness did God show us on the cross of Jesus Christ? What love! What mercy! What compassion! What pity!

GOD IS KIND TO ALL PEOPLE EVERYWHERE

Luke 6:35   *But love your enemies, and do good,*

and lend, expecting nothing in return, and your reward will be great, and you will be sons of the Most-High, for he is kind to the ungrateful and the evil.

Kindness and loving your enemies are very similar things. Kindness is having that inner disposition towards being a blessing to those who cannot or will not respond in kindness to you. Kindness is you being useful to someone else's well-being whether or not they are useful to your well-being. Kindness is not interested in being repaid. The Lord says that we should lend, expecting nothing in return. The Lord has just before this verse explained that wicked people love their friends. Wicked people help those who can repay them. But the Lord asks for something more than that from us. Love your enemies! Be kind to those who want to do harm to you. Lend to the ones who can never, or who will never, pay it back. Be useful toward someone else's well-fare or well-being. God is kind to everybody, even to the ungrateful and to the evil. And He says to us; be like Me in this.

GOD IS PARTICULARLY KIND TO THOSE WHOM HE SAVES

Ephesians 2:4-7   But God, being rich in mercy, because of the great love with which he loved us, 5 even when we were dead in our trespasses, made us alive together with Christ—by grace you have been saved— 6 and raised us up with him and seated us with him in the heavenly places in Christ Jesus, 7 so that in the coming ages he might show the immeasurable riches of his grace in kindness toward us in Christ Jesus.

God was rich in kindness towards us when we least deserved kindness. Why? So that He could be kind to us in the coming ages and ages forever! Look what the kindness of God does in Ephesians. It shows mercy. It actively loves the unlovable. It makes the dead come to life. It saves by pure grace. It raises the lowly ones up to be seated with Him in heavenly places. And then it spends eternity and all the coming ages pouring out more grace and more kindness!

DISCUSSION QUESTIONS:

1 – Here is a hypothetical situation. Someone is about to make a very bad decision. You explain to them that the choice they are making will lead them to very bad consequences. They ignore you and do it anyway. The result turns out exactly as you had predicted to them. They have put themselves into a very bad circumstance. Would you be inclined to help them out, or to let them live

with the consequences of their bad choice? What might God's inclination be? How has God dealt with you at such times?

2 - In what ways has God shown kindness to you?

3 – In Ephesians 2:7, we learn that God plans to show us the immeasurable riches of his grace in kindness toward us in Christ Jesus. And we learn that He plans to do this for ever. How does knowing this make you inclined to act toward others?

30 DAVID'S KINDNESS

God is kind and His Spirit is at work producing His kindness within us who believe. What exactly should the kindness of God at work in our lives look like? What should kindness, the fruit of the Spirit, look like in our actions? A Living Example of the Kindness of God as it is done by a human being could help us to get an idea of how this fruit of kindness may manifest in the people of God. This following scene takes place after David has been crowned as King over all Israel. He had just brought the Ark of the Covenant successfully into Jerusalem. He had defeated the Philistines, the Moabites, the Edomites, Amalekites, and the Ammonites. God had blessed David everywhere he turned and God had given him victory over all his enemies. The kingdom of Israel was now very firmly in David's hands. And after that is all accomplished, what does David think about?

II Samuel 9:1-8   And David said, "Is there still

anyone left of the house of Saul, that I may show him kindness for Jonathan's sake?" 2 Now there was a servant of the house of Saul whose name was Ziba, and they called him to David. And the king said to him, "Are you Ziba?" And he said, "I am your servant." 3 And the king said, "Is there not still someone of the house of Saul, that I may show the kindness of God to him?" Ziba said to the king, "There is still a son of Jonathan; he is crippled in his feet." 4 The king said to him, "Where is he?" And Ziba said to the king, "He is in the house of Machir the son of Ammiel, at Lo-debar." 5 Then King David sent and brought him from the house of Machir the son of Ammiel, at Lo-debar. 6 And Mephibosheth the son of Jonathan, son of Saul, came to David and fell on his face and paid homage. And David said, "Mephibosheth!" And he answered, "Behold, I am your servant." 7 And David said to him, "Do not fear, for I will show you kindness for the sake of your father Jonathan, and I will restore to you all the land of Saul your father, and you shall eat at my table always." 8 And he paid homage and said, "What is your servant, that you should show regard for a dead dog such as I?"

It is an interesting and very relevant fact that Saul was David's enemy. And yet it is Saul's house to whom David performs such kindness. There is a connection between kindness and loving your enemies. Saul tried repeatedly to kill David. Saul sent assassins after David to murder him. Saul himself threw a spear at David. He took his whole army out to hunt down and murder David. And despite all of this, David chooses to act with kindness toward Saul's remaining family. This is very Christ-like behavior. Jesus demonstrates God's kindness toward His enemies by laying down His life for them. God sent Jesus to us while we were still hostile towards Him. God showed His kindness toward us by sending us a Savior even while we hated Him and wanted nothing to do with Him. He saved us while we were His enemies (Romans 5:10). Kindness is something that is done on behalf of someone who may not deserve it or expect it. David was not required to show kindness to the house of Saul. He was in no way obligated to demonstrate kindness to the descendants of his enemy. No one was forcing David to do this. Yet he willingly and happily chose to be kind to Mephibosheth, the grandson of the man who hated him. Jesus demonstrates God's kindness because He gave His life for us willingly and not begrudgingly. Jesus said in John 10:18, "No one takes my life from Me, but I lay it down of myself." In other words, Jesus chose to die. He allowed Himself to be killed. He was not obligated to die for guilty sinners. No one forced Him to do it. Jesus **chose** to lay down His life so that others might live. The attitude behind an act of kindness is significant. The kindness becomes real on the outside only after it becomes real on the inside.

Another interesting and significant fact about David's act of kindness is that he didn't even know that Mephibosheth existed. David had to seek out the person to whom he would be kind. He actively sought to be kind to Mephibosheth. He had to ask questions and call servants and do some investigative digging, so that he could find a descendant of Saul to be kind to. I imagine it took a fair amount of seeking in order to be kind to someone in Saul's family, and yet David chose to put forth the effort. Jesus demonstrated God's kindness because He came to seek and save the lost (Luke 19:10). God did not wait for the lost to find Him, He went out seeking the lost in order to find them and bring them to Himself. This is the point of the parable of the lost sheep and the parable of the lost coin in Luke chapter fifteen. It is God who does the seeking and the finding of the lost, not the other way around. Kindness does not always wait to be asked. Kindness can be done even without being asked.

Kindness acts without regard to whether the one who is helped can ever repay the kindness. Mephibosheth was crippled. He was completely unable to take care of himself. He had to have help in order to live. He was totally dependent upon others for the basics of life. He could not work in the field. He could not work because he could not walk. Someone had to carry him or see to it that he got from place to place and David sees this as no barrier to his display of kindness. David welcomes Mephibosheth even though Mephibosheth will never be able to repay David for his kindness. Jesus demonstrated God's kindness by giving salvation away for free and expecting nothing in return. Titus 3:5 says, "he saved us, not because of works done by us in righteousness, but according to his own mercy." Acts of kindness are done without regard to the worthiness of the person and without regard to what that person may give one back. An act of kindness can stand alone without any external corresponding act in return.

DISCUSSION QUESTIONS:

1 – How is kindness like loving your enemies?

2 – Would you be willing to seek out someone to be kind to?

3 – Would you be willing to show kindness to someone who you know before hand will not show appreciation?

31 THE GOODNESS
OF GOD

THE FRUIT OF THE SPIRIT IS GOODNESS

> *Galatians 5:22-26   But the fruit of the Spirit
> is love, joy, peace, patience, kindness, goodness,
> faithfulness, 23 gentleness, self-control; against
> such things there is no law. 24 And those who
> belong to Christ Jesus have crucified the flesh with
> its passions and desires. 25 If we live by the Spirit,
> let us also keep in step with the Spirit. 26 Let
> us not become conceited, provoking one another,
> envying one another.*

The fruit of the Spirit is goodness. Those who
belong to Jesus Christ– those who are led by the
Spirit of God, have this fruit of goodness displayed
in their lives. The goodness of God is one of the
major, major standards of my life. The goodness of
God is one of the primary truths about God that I

cling to with all my strength. It is one of the things that you will have to try and pry out of my stubborn fingers because I would rather die than give it up. I will not let go of the truth of God's goodness. I will not surrender (with the help of God) the goodness of God. It is that important. We should all have some true things that are so precious to us that we will never surrender them. There ought to be some things that we are willing to die for.

During the days of the reformation, there were some guys who gave their lives over the issue of the right way and time to baptize people. I don't know if I would give my life over the issue of baptism. But the goodness of God, yes! Especially when you combine the goodness of God with the other doctrine that I feel like I could die for, which is the sovereignty of God.

I really don't mean to boast. I don't want to repeat the mistake of Peter and boast that I will stand with the Lord all the way until death. So, I will say that it is the ideal me who wants to be able to die for the truths of God. I am completely reliant on the strength that the Lord provides to get through even a normal day, let alone a life and death moment of truth. So, I am not trying to macho shame you into being brave and soldierly. I am just saying that there ought to be at least one or two hills upon which we take a stand, and where we say, here I draw the line. And for me, the goodness of God and the sovereignty of God are two of those hills. Because when you combine them together; they enable you to do anything, to face anything, and to endure anything.

Any time I am facing some difficulty, whenever I am dealing with some suffering, I preach these two truths to myself over and over again. God is good and God is sovereign. God is good and God is sovereign! And through these two, simple yet profound truths, I know - I absolutely know - that whatever is happening to me will be good for me and that God has permitted it to come upon me for that very purpose, for my good. These two guaranteed, always one hundred percent true things about God, when combined together, answer every question. They calm every fear, they dissolve every doubt, and they help us to get through any possible thing.

It happens sometimes that those who face pain and hardship in this life may doubt the goodness of God. But the clear message of Scripture is that God is good. In fact, the Bible describes God as being **uniquely good**, even to the point that He is the measure for everything that we call good. He is the very definition of good. He is, in fact, the very source of all that is good.

What does the goodness of God mean? Psalm 119:67 says this about God; "You are good and You do good." God's goodness can be defined as the collective perfections of His nature and the benevolence of His acts. God is good in His nature and God is good in what He does. God's goodness is one of His attributes, one of the basic things about Him which does not change. Psalm 107 says, "give thanks to the Lord because He IS good."

Hosea 3:5   Afterward the children of Israel shall return and seek the Lord their God, and David their king, and they shall come in fear to the Lord and to his goodness in the latter days.

The goodness of God so permeates who He is that Hosea says coming to God is coming to His goodness. There is no separation between God and goodness. So, not only is goodness an attribute of God, but it is a quality that is enmeshed and interwoven into all of His other attributes. So that whatever God is – that is a good thing. And whatever God does is a good thing. So that even the wrath of God is a good wrath. Some even argue that God's goodness is the sum total of all His attributes, so that you cannot have goodness without God, and you cannot have God without goodness.

Psalm 16:2   I say to the Lord, "You are my Lord; I have no good apart from you."

God is the source of everything that is good.

> *James 1:17   Every good gift and every perfect gift is from above, coming down from the Father of lights, with whom there is no variation or shadow due to change.*

EVERYTHING GOD DOES IS GOOD

This truth is a challenge to those who question God's goodness when they consider the many bad things that can happen in life. They say, "Why does God allow bad things to happen if He is so good?" "Why do innocent people die if God is so good?"

An important thing for us to understand is that God is not responsible for all the bad things which take place on the earth. Even though God is sovereign and in control of everything, another important truth is relevant to the disasters of life – man's responsibility. Galatians tells us that whatever a man sows that is what he will reap. This means that often the bad things that happen to us are brought about by our own stubbornness, willfulness and sin. And even if we are not able to define a clear connection between a sinful act and some ensuing disaster, the entire earth is under a curse that was brought about by man's original sin. Being steeped in sinfulness, it is inevitable that bad things will happen to anyone and everyone who lives on the earth. The entire planet is awash in sin and its evil consequences. Even earthquakes, hurricanes and other "natural" disasters have their roots in the sinfulness of mankind. These disasters were never a part of the original plan, but are brought about by the curse on the earth due to sin. Crime, political turmoil, floods – literally everything bad that happens and that can happen is the result of sin. When the Lord finished his creation, He declared that it was all very good (Genesis 1:31). It was not until sin came into the world that the earth developed its current problems. Therefore, the evil in creation must be attributed to someone other than God. He is sovereign and in control of everything, but evil cannot be attributed to him.

> *James 1:13   Let no one say when he is tempted, "I am tempted by God"; for God cannot be tempted by evil, nor does He Himself tempt anyone.*

However, although God is not the author of evil, he nonetheless uses all things, including evil, for his glory. God cannot be held accountable, He cannot be blamed for anything evil, or even for anything that is not good. But He can take the evil that is done and cause good things to come out of it.

> *Genesis 50:19-20   Joseph said to them, "Do not be afraid, for am I in the place of God? 20 But as for you, you meant evil against me; but God meant it for good, in order to bring it about as it is this day, to save many people alive.*

Joseph's brothers were jealous of him and sold him as a slave. That was an evil act on the part of his brothers. It was indeed very evil, very much not good, but God used that evil act to put Joseph in the place where he could save millions of people from starvation. He cannot be blamed for any evil thing that happens in our world. In fact, He very often decreases the impact of the evil actions of others, and even turns the impact completely around, as he did in the life of Joseph. And since God is good, since God is the standard for what is good, since His goodness permeates all; then all that He is is good, and everything God does is good.

DISCUSSION QUESTIONS:

1 – Describe how God's goodness means that everything that He does is good.

2 - Describe why the goodness of God does not

mean that nothing bad happens in this world.

3 – Describe how good is called evil and evil is called good in our world today. Give some examples.

32 THE MISUNDERSTOOD GOODNESS OF GOD

Sometimes people very much like us may look at their personal circumstances, or maybe at the general conditions of the world, and begin to wonder where in all this mess is the famous goodness of God? There are times when the goodness of God, even as it is at work in our lives, seems kind of invisible. There are times when what is happening to us does not feel so good. We quote to ourselves Romans 8:28, saying "all things work together for good for those who love God, who are called according to His purposes." We quote that famous, popular verse to ourselves, and yet, what we are experiencing doesn't quite feel like what the words say.

I think a good way to describe and illustrate how this can happen is to look at Psalm seventy-three. Apart from the divine revelation of the Scriptures, we cannot recognize true goodness, because it cannot be understood apart from knowing God and seeing life from His perspective. This is precisely the point of Psalm seventy-three. At least it is one of the points of the Psalm. Asaph, who was the chief musician under David, wrote the Psalm. The first and the last verses of the psalm contain the word "good." Through the course of time in the psalm, Asaph undergoes a radical change in his understanding of the meaning of the term "good," as it applies to the goodness of God. Because Asaph's misconceptions about the goodness of God are virtually the same that many Christians have today, we might want to understand the message of this psalm. Asaph describes a period in his life when he had serious spiritual struggles over his understanding of the goodness of God.

> *Psalm 73:1-3   Truly God is good to Israel, to those who are pure in heart. 2 But as for me, my feet had almost stumbled, my steps had nearly slipped. 3 For I was envious of the arrogant when I saw the prosperity of the wicked.*

Asaph's view of the goodness of God at the beginning of the Psalm can be seen in verse one. "God is good to Israel, to those who are pure in heart." In other words, God was good to good people, but not good to bad people. God was good toward His chosen people and would bless them. But He would certainly not allow evil people to prosper and be at ease. The expectation this created in Asaph was that God would bestow blessings on the people of Israel, like himself; and the Lord would bestow curses on the wicked people who did not know Him. But this view of the goodness of God did not compute with what Asaph observed in the world around him. And it would not compute with our observations of the world around us either. We see the wicked prospering everywhere. And we likewise see the godly suffering on a large scale. So, Asaph's conception of what it means for God to be good was a bit off, and this was actually leading him to a place of stumbling and losing his faith. He says, "my feet had almost stumbled, my steps had nearly slipped." So then, his wrong doctrine, which was that the people of God prosper and the wicked people suffer, was causing him to stumble. And it was causing him to stumble because simple observation of the world proved that his premise was simply not true. A lot of good people, godly people, suffer. While at the same time many wicked people seemed to have it pretty good. This view of the blessing and cursing of God did not match the reality that Asaph could easily see with his own eyes. In verse four, Asaph says the wicked people don't even suffer when they die. Their death is even easier than the death of godly people. In verse five the wicked people don't have troubles like us godly people do. The wicked seem so arrogant and so powerful and so in charge of life.

Psalm 73:6-9   Therefore pride is their necklace; violence covers them as a garment. 7 Their eyes swell out through fatness; their hearts overflow with follies. 8 They scoff and speak with malice; loftily they threaten oppression. 9 They set their mouths against the heavens, and their tongue struts through the earth.

Look at what Asaph saw in the pride of the wicked. And really, his observations were true. Pride is their necklace. They wear their pride openly, like an ornament – an accessory. They are violent. Their hearts overflow with foolishness. They scoff and speak with malice. They don't have gentle words for anyone. "They set their mouths against the heavens, and their tongue struts through the earth." Asaph was heart-broken by the arrogance of the proud and wicked. He saw them strutting and posturing in a victorious way, as if the things they did had no consequences whatsoever. As Asaph sees these things it brings him to a kind of despair. It makes him think that maybe this life of serving God is not worth it. It seems to have more negatives than positives.

Psalm 73:13-14   All in vain have I kept my heart

clean and washed my hands in innocence. 14 For all the day long I have been stricken and rebuked every morning.

"I am the one who gets punished every day," Asaph thinks. "Even though I strive to be good, I am the one who gets the most rebukes from God. I am the one who gets the worst of this life. Even though I struggle to keep my heart clean, even though I strive to guard over my thoughts to keep them holy, even though I wash my hands non-stop; it is me who experiences the greater difficulties. Is the law of sowing and reaping broken? It sure doesn't seem to be functioning properly. Am I doing all of this in vain?" You see how the wrong understanding of what it means for God to be good will lead to despair and confusion of faith? Some contemporary examples of misunderstanding what it means for God to be good could be...

(One) The idea that God prospers the godly people with this world's stuff and takes material blessings away from the wicked. This is the same misunderstanding that Asaph had. There is nothing new under the sun. We know that this misunderstanding leads to the prosperity gospel, which itself leads to despair and to a dead end.

(Two) That the goodness of God means that He will certainly heal all of His people who trust Him from every sickness. We know this misunderstanding leads to believers concluding that if they just had more faith, they would have no suffering. When a friend of mine lost his wife to cancer, a fellow church-goer at the funeral rebuked him for not having enough faith to get his wife healed. What an evil thing to say to a grieving man.

Asaph admits to his readers that he strayed far off course. He was so far from the truth that he came close to destruction. In his own words, "his feet had almost slipped." He seems to be confessing that he considered giving up the faith and forsaking the idea of godly living, thinking that it was of no real benefit. Asaph's problem was largely due to his distorted perspective. Asaph had been envying the wicked. While Lot was living in a terribly sinful city, the Bible tells us that he was vexed, deeply troubled, by the sin all around him (II Peter 2:7-8). While Asaph did not approve of the evil actions of the wicked people around him, he was more disturbed by seeing and envying their prosperity than he was by their sin. Asaph wished he could be in the shoes of those who were wicked. He did not hate their sin; he envied their success.

Asaph also suffered from self-righteousness. He looked at himself as being better than he was. He seems to have believed that he somehow deserved God's blessings more than the "wicked" people deserved it. And so, he concluded that his "righteous living" had been for nothing.

Psalm 73:13-14   All in vain have I kept my heart clean and washed my hands in innocence. 14 For all the day long I have been stricken and rebuked every morning.

These verses also suggest Asaph viewed his suffering as coming from God. He thought God was punishing him for being godly. Asaph seems to have been consumed with self-pity. It is really difficult to see life clearly when you are looking at it through tears of self-pity.

So, seeing the danger that his view of things had put him in, Asaph decides to pray and seek God's wisdom. Then the light turns on and he sees God's approach to things more clearly. He sees that the wicked people do not actually have it so good. They are not actually in such a good place as it seems they are. He sees that their success actually does great harm to them, and puts them in danger.

Psalm 73:18-20   Truly you set them in slippery places; you make them fall to ruin. 19 How they are destroyed in a moment, swept away utterly by terrors! 20 Like a dream when one awakes, O Lord, when you rouse yourself, you despise them as phantoms.

Those who seemed to be doing so well in their wickedness, Asaph now saw as being in great danger. Their feet were on a slippery place. They were on a steep slope that could only bring them down into terrors. In just a short time, they would face the judgment of God. Their payday for sin might not come in this life, but it was surely coming. Their apparently blessed condition at the time was not an indictor of eternal good to come. In fact, just the opposite was true. Their current blessings served to blind them to their eternal needs. They lived solely for the here and now, and were careless for God's things.

> Psalm 73:21-22   When my soul was embittered, when I was pricked in heart, 22 I was brutish and ignorant; I was like a beast toward you.

And now he sees how foolish he was to doubt God's goodness. He saw that the conditions he lived in at any given time in life did not necessarily represent God's goodness or un-goodness. It wasn't such a simple thing that the godly would prosper and the wicked would suffer. And Asaph admits that his old understanding of things was kind of brutish and ignorant, without true wisdom. "I was like a beast," he says. But finally, now, Asaph gets an eternal perspective on things.

Psalm 73:23-26   Nevertheless, I am continually with you; you hold my right hand. 24 You guide me with your counsel, and afterward you will receive me to glory. 25 Whom have I in heaven but you? And there is nothing on earth that I desire besides you. 26 My flesh and my heart may fail, but God is the strength of my heart and my portion forever.

He is no longer so concerned with the "right now" conditions of life. And that is because he has gained an eternal perspective. He says that "after this life you will receive me into glory. And besides that, there is nothing on earth that I really want compared to You, Lord. You are my strength and my portion forever! I am done chasing after these things of the earth that I thought were pure blessings, because now I know that the real blessing is to be kept near to you, O God."

Psalm 73:27-28   For behold, those who are far from you shall perish; you put an end to everyone who is unfaithful to you. 28 But for me it is good to be near God; I have made the Lord God my refuge, that I may tell of all your works.

Early in the Psalm, the goodness of God toward Asaph meant that life on earth would be smooth and without difficulties. But by the end of the Psalm the goodness of God toward Asaph meant that God would do in his life whatever it took to keep Asaph close to Him. How foolish Asaph's thinking had been – like the thoughts of a beast, an animal who falls easily into a trap. How foolish he had been to think that the wicked would get away with their sin, and there would be no day of reckoning. How foolish Asaph was to come to the conclusion that God was punishing him for avoiding the sinful ways of the wicked.

Asaph now sees his relationship with God in its true light. Eternity holds for him the bright hope of God's glorious, presence. Asaph also sees his "affliction," whatever that might be, as a source of great blessing. His suffering drew him closer to God, while the prosperity of the wicked drew them away from God. His trials were in reality a gift from God for Asaph's good. His struggles had led him into a deeper intimacy with God and so they were worth all the pain and distress. Now Asaph understands the "goodness" of God in a different way. He has a new definition for "good." In verse one, "good" really meant the absence of pain, difficulty, trouble, sorrow, bad health, or poverty. In verse twenty-eight, "good" means something far better than physical prosperity:

Psalm 73:28   But for me it is good to be near God;

*I have made the Lord God my refuge, that I may
tell of all your works.*

Nearness to God, intimate fellowship with God, is our highest good. We can safely say then that whatever interferes with our nearness to God, our fellowship with Him, is actually evil and bad for us. For some of us to have a bunch of money would be deadly to our faith. For some of us, a life of ease would be catastrophic and have a bad end. And whatever draws us into a deeper fellowship with God is actually "good." Even if it feels bad at the time.

When God brings suffering and adversity into our lives, our confidence in His goodness should not be undermined. Instead, we should be reassured of His goodness to us. In the end, Job's suffering brought him nearer to God - therefore it was good, and God was good in afflicting him. Paul's suffering brought him nearer to God, and he saw it as a blessing (Philippians 3:10). The chastening of the Lord in the life of the Christian is not only evidence of our sonship, it is God's working in us for good (Hebrews 12:1-13, Romans 8:28). So, for us to have a right understanding of the goodness of God, we need to have the long view. We need to have a grasp on how things will play out over the long haul. We need to have eternity in our hearts.

DISCUSSION QUESTIONS:

1 – Does the Bible promise to make all of the Lord's followers healthy and wealthy?

2 – Describe how a misunderstanding of the goodness of God could lead someone to a confusion of faith.

3 – Discuss different ways that you recognize the goodness of God on your behalf where the goodness felt uncomfortable or painful.

33 WHAT BEARING THE FRUIT OF GOODNESS LOOKS LIKE

If we are bearing the fruit of goodness, what will that look like? It means that we will have benevolent attitudes toward others, and that we will act toward them in ways that are good for them. It also means that we will act in general in a way that is good, and this will be fairly evident for others to see. There will be some consistency to our Christian behavior. There will be a steady brightness to our lamp of truth. We will be...

GOOD TREES

Luke 6:43-45 "For no good tree bears bad fruit, nor again does a bad tree bear good fruit, 44 for each tree is known by its own fruit. For figs are not gathered from thornbushes, nor are grapes picked from a bramble bush. 45 The* *good person out of the good treasure of his heart produces good, and the evil person out of his evil treasure produces evil, for out of the abundance of the heart his mouth speaks.*

The nature of the tree determines the quality of the fruit. If the goodness of God is really in us then it will show in what we do and in what we say. The Lord ends verse forty-five by telling us that a good person will be one whose spoken words reflect their inner condition. What we do and what we say reflect who we are. The more the Holy Spirit takes up residence in our lives, the more we let Him lead us, the more we will behave and speak like the Lord. This "good tree," "bad tree" illustration of the Lord's reflects the same idea we saw in Psalm 119:68. Talking of God, it says two things; You are good, and You do good. The doing comes out of the being. Goodness is first of all what you are. It is the nature of the tree to be good or not good. A tree that is planted by God cannot help but yield good fruit, eventually. Your actions will accord with your nature, as will your words. "Out of the abundance of the heart the mouth speaks."

As we are transformed over time, as our nature falls more in line with the Holy Spirit who guides us, we will be increasingly good in our obvious behavior and in the core of who we are. Will there be letdowns? Will there be relapses into the old behavior? Yes, there will be. But there will be an upward trajectory of progress. It has to be so because of Philippians 1:6. "He who began a good work in you will bring it to completion." We will be...

SALT AND LIGHT

In the sermon on the mount, Jesus tells us what it will mean for us to live as those who are under His rule, as His disciples. The sermon on the mount is like a description of what the people are like who submit to God and live under His care and His leadership.

> *Matthew 5:13-16*   *"You are the salt of the earth, but if salt has lost its taste, how shall its saltiness be restored? It is no longer good for anything except to be thrown out and trampled under people's feet. 14 "You are the light of the world. A city set on a hill cannot be hidden. 15 Nor do people light a lamp and put it under a basket, but on a stand, and it gives light to all in the house. 16 In the same way, let your light shine before others, so that they may see your good works and give glory to your Father who is in heaven.*

The life of those who are disciples of Jesus will be like salt. Their lives will be like salt in the sense that salt was used to stop meat or fish from getting rotten. Salt counteracted the natural process of decay and corruption. So, in a world that is marked by the rotting decay and corruption of sin, the people of God are people who avoid personal corruption. Our lives as His ambassadors are to present an alternative to the world's usual and normal modes of living. Jesus told us that we are the light of the world. What did He mean by that? Did He mean that we were to be lamps in the sense that we ought to be preaching the good news to the world? Are we called the light of the world because of the words we speak to them? Yes, in part. But look at the way He finishes this analogy. He says, "You are the light of the world. You guys illuminate the place. You are here like a lamp set in a dark place. How do you let your light shine? You let your light shine by letting others see your good works, so that they will give glory to the Father who is in heaven." Your life and my life ought to be lived in such a way that others are attracted to God when they see our good works and will then desire to glorify God in the same way. How can our lives be attractive like that? They need to be filled with goodness, mercy. Kindness, patience, long-suffering, compassion, love and justice. The fruit of goodness is evident when the people around us see our good works.

Isaiah 58:6-10   *"Is not this the fast that I*

choose: to loose the bonds of wickedness, to undo
the straps of the yoke, to let the oppressed go free,
and to break every yoke? 7 Is it not to share your
bread with the hungry and bring the homeless
poor into your house; when you see the naked, to
cover him, and not to hide yourself from your own
flesh? 8 Then shall your light break forth like the
dawn, and your healing shall spring up speedily;
your righteousness shall go before you; the glory
of the Lord shall be your rear guard. 9 Then you
shall call, and the Lord will answer; you shall cry,
and he will say, 'Here I am.' If you take away the
yoke from your midst, the pointing of the finger,
and speaking wickedness, 10 if you pour yourself
out for the hungry and satisfy the desire of the
afflicted, then shall your light rise in the darkness
and your gloom be as the noonday.

Here in Isaiah, your light shines by doing good things for others. By helping them get free from the bonds of wickedness. By sharing your bread with the hungry. By bringing the homeless poor into your house. By covering the naked. By not hiding yourself from the needs of others. Then your light will break forth like the dawn. God is good. And some of His goodness can leak out to the world through us as we mature in the faith, making it possible for God to be good to others through us. And this is a bigger deal than you might think. To have the character of God expressed to others through you is a miraculous and profound thing.

I don't care what great and grand things a person may accomplish in life. Without the fruit of the Spirit being present in us, we are doing nothing of lasting value.

DISCUSSION QUESTIONS:

1 – Explain what it means that a good tree bears good fruit and a bad tree bears bad fruit.

2 – Describe what it means for a Christian to be salt and light.

3 – Describe a time when you saw good fruit in someone's life, and seeing that made you desire to be like them.

34 WHAT IS GENTLENESS

Galatians 5:22-25   But the fruit of the Spirit is love, joy, peace, patience, kindness, goodness, faithfulness, 23 gentleness, self-control; against such things there is no law. 24 And those who belong to Christ Jesus have crucified the flesh with its passions and desires. 25 If we live by the Spirit, let us also keep in step with the Spirit.

The fruit of the Spirit is gentleness. What is gentleness, exactly? Is being gentle like being soft and calm and unthreatening? Is being gentle being weak and harmless? If so, that's kind of an unattractive trait. If you think of gentleness as a sort of mild-mannered powerlessness, then it is not something that most of us, especially men, would desire to strive for. I met a guy in high school who belonged to an interesting club. The club was called the Dependent Order of Really Meek and Timid Souls (DOORMATS). To me, that did not seem like a good group to join. And I don't think that particular idea of gentleness really hits the mark that the Bible is trying to show us.

In seeking to define exactly what gentleness is in this passage, I needed to do some research. Since I am not a Greek guy, since I am not learned in the Greek language, I have to depend on the experts who are knowledgeable about Greek. And what they say about this word for gentleness here is that it has no matching English word. It does not have a direct word it can be translated into. There is no corresponding English word, but the words gentleness or meekness probably come the closest to the original. Most English translations choose one of those two words in Galatians. The KJV and the American Standard Version use meekness, while the ESV, the NASB and the NKJV use gentleness.

The ancient Greeks defined it like this...

> (ONE) Gentleness or meekness describes persons or things which have in them a certain soothing quality. For example, having a humble and kind demeanor which calms another's anger. So here, gentleness is something that can somehow bring the temperature of a hot situation down.

> (TWO) Gentleness describes a way of behavior that is surprisingly calm or peaceful, especially on the part of people who had it in their power to act otherwise. For example, a king

forgiving a servant who failed him in some way. The king has the authority and power to render punishment, but chooses instead to show kindness and forgiveness. Such a king would be praised for his "gentle" behavior. So, gentleness is a kind of a holding back one's authority or power over another.

(THREE) Gentleness is the ability to take unkind remarks with a good nature. For example, when in a heated discussion if your opponent stoops to name calling, but you refuse to stoop down to their level and do the same. So, gentleness is like holding back anger.

(FOUR) Gentleness is a combination of strength and restraint. For example, a horse that is obedient to the reins. A horse is a huge and powerful animal, and yet they can be controlled by reins. There is great strength present, but it is restrained, tempered by a gentle spirit.

So then, gentleness is something like strength that is under control, or anger that is being tempered. Gentleness is power that is being restrained. Gentleness is authority that is being held in check. Which means that meekness is not weakness. Gentleness is not being a doormat. Gentleness is not the lack of strength. It is great strength that is under control.

When I was a little boy, we had a 250lb St. Bernard named Zacharias. A friend visited us one day with their Chihuahua puppy. That little puppy began to play with Zacharias. Zach was laying down on the floor with his head up, and that little puppy with those sharp, puppy teeth would actually jump up and grab Zach's ear and hang there, dangling beside Zach's giant head. Zach was not happy. But he was very gentle with the puppy, leaning his head over and gently pushing the puppy off of his ear with his huge paw. Eventually he just put one paw on top of the puppy and held him down on the floor to keep him under control. Gentleness is strength that is under control. Gentleness is strength that does no harm.

But don't mistake gentleness that does no harm with gentleness that does nothing. You can correct your child in a gentle way. You can steer your child away from a bad course in life and toward a good course in life in a gentle way. You can take many strong actions in a gentle manner.

Thinking about the gentleness of God as He deals with us, many of us would probably understand that God deals with us in as gentle a way as He possibly can, while still anchoring us in the truth. He will exert just enough force from His unlimited power to get the job done. But He will manage to be gentle with us in the process of directing us. We see this forceful gentleness in the way the Lord deals with Israel when He sends them as exiles to Babylon. Jeremiah chapter twenty-nine is a letter sent by the prophet Jeremiah to the exiles.

In the letter he tells them, "Ok, you are prisoners now. But don't fight it, don't rebel against it. Let this thing that I am putting you through do its perfect work. Live there, work there and marry there. Work for the good of the city where I am sending you. I will not let you suffer too much, and in seventy years the work I am doing in you will be done, and I will bring you back home. I am not doing this to harm you (my paraphrase)." In this letter to the exiles is the very popular verse...

> Jeremiah 29:11   For I know the plans I have for you, declares the Lord, plans for welfare and not for evil, to give you a future and a hope.

This is God's great power being exerted on the people in a gentle way to bring about some good for them. I think this is a good way to understand gentleness; it is power or authority that is used in a way that does no harm. It is authority or power or even anger, that is held in control so that a good outcome is achieved with no harm.

Gentleness is really lacking in our culture and in the world at large. I will frequently read a variety of debates on twitter between hundreds of people. Often the participants in the debates are not gentle with each other. Especially in political debates. One person will make his point, and then the response usually goes something like this; "Well, since you are so stupid, I will explain it to you like I would to a child." And then the response to the response goes something like this, "My child knows more about this than you, you pathetic blankety-blank!" And on it goes. So, our world could use some wise and timely gentleness.

Gentleness has a crucial role to play in Christian life. It is a key tool in the discipleship tool bag. It is absolutely essential in Christian leaders. And Christian gentleness will provide a nice alternative to the world by being a living contrast to the epidemic of anger and brutality that is out there. Gentleness is not really the absence of anger, but it is having the right kind of anger in the right quantity and for the right duration of time. Gentleness is the virtue that sort of tempers our anger. If we suffer some injustice or if we see some injustice, gentleness keeps our anger under control, while still seeking to address the injustice. Gentleness is the moderation of anger, not the absence, of anger. Gentleness is like being angry in the right way, in a non-destructive way. Being angry in the wrong way would be like exploding on a person with unkind words or violence. Of course, that is an obviously bad anger.

Another kind of bad anger is the completely unexpressed anger, the "pretend it is not there," kind of anger - the "pretend nothing is happening" kind of anger. The person who is "cool with everything," who is never disagreeable, who always compliments and never criticizes, is not necessarily gentle. There are some things we should not put up with for the sake of "keeping the peace." Gentleness is the virtuous middle road between cruel anger (anger in excess) and unexpressed anger. Gentleness is opposed to all forms of prideful anger: "quarreling, jealousy, anger, hostility." But gentleness is also opposed to turning a blind eye to the problem. There are some cases where a failure to be angry is a failure to respond in the right way. In other words, there are some cases where the failure to be rightly angry is a failure of courage to do the right thing.

Gentleness is not opposed to all forms of anger. The gentle or meek person does not forsake all desire for vengeance when they are wronged. That is an impossible ideal, not a true biblical meekness or gentleness. The meek or gentle person entrusts vengeance to the Lord and, out of love for the offender, hopes and prays for the conversion and reconciliation of the offender.

> *Romans 12:19-21   Beloved, never avenge yourselves, but leave it to the wrath of God, for it is written, "Vengeance is mine, I will repay, says the Lord." 20 To the contrary, "if your enemy is hungry, feed him; if he is thirsty, give him something to drink; for by so doing, you will heap burning coals on his head." 21 Do not be overcome*

by evil, but overcome evil with good.

The gentle person is still interested in justice being done. They are just willing to leave all justice in the hands of God. A gentle person can resist the urge to self-defend. But, in circumstances where God's honor or our neighbor's good are at stake, holding back our anger might be sinful. There is such a thing as righteous anger.

DISCUSSION QUESSTIONS:

1 – Describe a circumstance where gentleness can have a soothing quality which brings down the tension or anxiety in the room.

2 – Describe a situation where gentleness is like great strength or authority that is under control.

3 – Describe a situation where responding with righteous anger is more appropriate than staying silent.

35 THE GENTLENESS
OF GOD

Before we look for the gentleness of God in the scriptures, let's look at one of seemingly less gentle, and more awesome moments.

> *Exodus 19:16-19*   *On the morning of the third day there were thunders and lightnings and a thick cloud on the mountain and a very loud trumpet blast, so that all the people in the camp trembled. 17 Then Moses brought the people out of the camp to meet God, and they took their stand at the foot of the mountain. 18 Now Mount Sinai was wrapped in smoke because the Lord had descended on it in fire. The smoke of it went up like the smoke of a kiln, and the whole mountain trembled greatly. 19 And as the sound of the trumpet grew louder and louder, Moses spoke, and God answered him in thunder.*

This scene is a fearsome one. The flashes

of lightening and the thick clouds of smoke for the eyes to see, the heavy peals of thunder and the loud trumpet blasts for the ears to hear. The whole mountain on fire, with the smoke rising in thick darkness. The mountain trembling as if there was a great earthquake happening. The people themselves all trembled in the fear of God. Certainly, He presented Himself to the people in a majestic and powerful way in this scene at Mount Sinai. Ever louder trumpet blasts came out of the boiling, chaotic mountain. Nothing about this moment felt very gentle to the people. When Moses spoke to God, God answered in thunder. I think of this place, Mount Sinai, as the place of the law's sternness. The law is given in this place, and the law can seem very harsh, very demanding. It is intensely serious and filled with dire consequence. The law shines a bright light on sin and its guilt. We hear the voice of thundering, and we see the flashing of lightning. Clouds and darkness and all dreadfulness surround the mountain. The people are kept far away because of the fearful holiness of the place. No one thinks of hearing anything gentle at Mount Sinai. And yet, it was on this same mountain where we hear God speak of Himself as He allows Moses to see Him.

Exodus 34:6-7a   The Lord passed before him and proclaimed, "The Lord, the Lord, a God merciful and gracious, slow to anger, and abounding in steadfast love and faithfulness, 7 keeping steadfast love for thousands, forgiving iniquity and transgression and sin

The gentleness of God is put on display for us to see in a kind of contrast with the power of God. A thick, dark cloud covers the mountain, the ground trembles at the presence of God. There is loud thunder, flashes of lightening - great power on display. And on that same mountain, a short time later, we hear God proclaimed as "merciful, gracious, slow to anger, and abounding in steadfast love and faithfulness, keeping steadfast love for thousands, forgiving iniquity and transgression and sin." I think this is a very truthful display of the gentleness of God. Gentleness is by no means a weakness. There is first this grand display of power and authority, and then there are the declarations of gentleness. In the shadow of the great power, we see the mercy and graciousness. The slowness to anger and the steadfast love, and the great forgiveness are there with the awesome power and authority. Another great biblical example of the gentleness of God can be seen in the life of Elijah.

I Kings 19:9-14   There he came to a cave and lodged in it. And behold, the word of the Lord came to him, and he said to him,

"What are you doing here, Elijah?" 10 He said, "I have been very jealous for the Lord, the God of hosts. For the people of Israel have forsaken your covenant, thrown down your altars, and killed your prophets with the sword, and I, even I only, am left, and they seek my life, to take it away." 11 And he said, "Go out and stand on the mount before the Lord." And behold, the Lord passed by, and a great and strong wind tore the mountains and broke in pieces the rocks before the Lord, but the Lord was not in the wind. And after the wind an earthquake, but the Lord was not in the earthquake. 12 And after the earthquake a fire, but the Lord was not in the fire. And after the fire the sound of a low whisper. 13 And when Elijah heard it, he wrapped his face in his cloak and went out and stood at the entrance of the cave. And behold, there came a voice to him and said, "What are you doing here, Elijah?" 14 He said, "I have been very jealous for the Lord, the God of hosts. For the people of Israel have forsaken your covenant, thrown down your altars, and killed your prophets with the sword, and I, even I only, am left, and they seek my life, to take it away.

God's power again was displayed in three ways; in a great, strong wind, in an earthquake and in a fire.   Verse eleven says this "behold, the Lord passed by, and a great and strong wind tore the mountains and broke in pieces the rocks before the Lord, but the Lord was not in the wind." And then it says, "And after the wind an earthquake, but the Lord was not in the earthquake." And verse twelve says, "And after the earthquake a fire, but the Lord was not in the fire." What does it mean that the Lord was not in the wind? What does it mean that the Lord was not in the earthquake? What does it mean that the Lord was not in the fire? God is teaching Elijah, and us, something here about His gentleness, about His slowness to anger, about His great patience.

Remember, Elijah had run here to this mountain place in fear for his life. He ran from the tornado or the hurricane that was Jezebel. He ran from the fiery earthquake that was her anger. And he was feeling pretty sorry for himself. "I am the only one," he said. "All the others have forsaken you, Lord. I was very jealous for you, but they have all abandoned you." Just because Jezebel wants to kill you doesn't mean you are the only one still serving God. God never leaves Himself without a witness. He tells Elijah that just in Jerusalem alone He has 7,000 faithful people. Not to mention all the others scattered throughout the country. You are not the only one, and you are never really alone.

God shows that He could easily speak to Elijah or us in these powerful, earth-shaking and intimidating ways, but He does not choose to – at least not all the time. He chooses instead to speak in the gentle whispering voice. Poor Elijah thinks it all depends on Him, and maybe the fact that the people of the world are allowed to speak to Elijah in such an ungentle way makes him feel more alone. Elijah does not need to worry. God has got everything firmly under control, and He can do it all with a gentleness. God doesn't feel the need to bring fire down from heaven every day to prove Himself. I think Elijah would like it if He did. So might most of us. But because of the gentleness of God, He doesn't always express His strength, but He restrains it, keeping it under control, speaking with gentleness instead.

Elijah Himself had gotten used to calling down fire from heaven. Once when he had his duel with the prophets of Baal, and twice when Ahab's soldiers were hunting him down, fire came down to vindicate God and Elijah. Everything doesn't have to be a turn or burn moment. Sometimes God works through his gentle persuasion in speaking to His people. And God is so gentle with Elijah that He gives him just three more things to do.

> *I Kings 19:15-16   And the Lord said to him, "Go, return on your way to the wilderness of Damascus. And when you arrive, you shall anoint Hazael to be king over Syria. 16 And Jehu the son of Nimshi you shall anoint to be king over Israel, and Elisha the son of Shaphat of Abelmeholah you shall anoint to be prophet in your place.*

The Lord tells Elijah to do these three things. First, go to Damascus to anoint Hazael to be king over Syria. Second, go back to Israel and anoint Jehu to be king instead of Ahab. And then last go find Elisha and anoint him to be prophet after you. I think the Lord knows that Elijah is tired, so He gives him only these three things to do until his time on the earth is finished. The Lord is very gentle with Elijah. And just like that, Jesus is gentle with us.

Matthew 11:28-30   Come to me, all who labor and are heavy laden, and I will give you rest. 29 Take my yoke upon you, and learn from me, for I am gentle and lowly in heart, and you will find rest for your souls. 30 For my yoke is easy, and my burden is light."

"I know your burden," the Lord says. "I know your troubles. I know how hard you are laboring under your burdens. I know that you are carrying a heavy load. I am gentle. I am lowly of heart. I will not stomp on you. I won't break you. I will put a yoke on you, but it will be an easy one. And your burden will be lighter than it is now." Look at Jesus during His trial displaying an amazing meekness.

Matthew 27:12-14   But when he was accused by the chief priests and elders, he gave no answer. 13 Then Pilate said to him, "Do you not hear how many things they testify against you?" 14 But he gave him no answer, not even to a single charge, so that the governor was greatly amazed.

Isaiah 53:7   He was oppressed, and he was afflicted, yet he opened not his mouth; like a lamb that is led to the slaughter, and like a sheep that before its shearers is silent, so he opened not his mouth.

He was not silent out of weakness. He had no intention of defending Himself. He was here to be crucified. He was here to give His life, not to preserve it. He could have called ten legions of angels to come to Him and fight. He could display strength, and He often did.

John 2:14-17   In the temple he found those who were selling oxen and sheep and pigeons, and the money-changers sitting there. 15 And making a whip of cords, he drove them all out of the temple, with the sheep and oxen. And he poured out the coins of the money-changers and overturned their tables. 16 And he told those who sold the pigeons, "Take these things away; do not make my Father's house a house of trade." 17 His disciples remembered that it was written, "Zeal for your house will consume me."

Even our salvation depended on His gentleness. David said of God, "your gentleness has made me great." Not one of us will ever be great without gentleness. He humbled Himself and became a mere man. Even though He was equal with God, He did not cling to that, but humbled Himself to become one of us. And He displayed His gentleness for all to see, choosing to save us by sacrificing Himself instead of coming with brute force to subdue us all and force us to obey.

> Zechariah 9:9   Rejoice greatly, O daughter of Zion! Shout aloud, O daughter of Jerusalem! Behold, your king is coming to you; righteous and having salvation is he, humble and mounted on a donkey, on a colt, the foal of a donkey.

He is not riding on a warhorse to trample over you. He is coming gently to visit His people and give His life for them. Later He will come on a war horse. Then He will trample the winepress of the wrath of God.

DISCUSSION QUESTIONS:

1 – Does God's dealings with the people of Israel and Moses at Mount Sinai convince you of the gentleness of God? What do you think would cause

someone with all power to act in a gentle way?

2 – In the passages from Matthew 24 and Isaiah 53 above, why do you think Jesus did not speak to defend Himself?

3 – Explain how our salvation depends on the gentleness of God.

36 OUR CALL TO GENTLENESS

GENTLENESS AS PART OF A WORTHY WALK

Ephesians 4:1-3   I therefore, a prisoner for the Lord, urge you to walk in a manner worthy of the calling to which you have been called, 2 with all humility and gentleness, with patience, bearing with one another in love, 3 eager to maintain the unity of the Spirit in the bond of peace.

Paul tells us to live a life that is worthy of the calling to which we have been called. We have been called to live a life as ambassadors representing the kingdom of God. And how do we live in a manner worthy of this calling? We live with these qualities visible in our lives; humility, gentleness, patience, bearing with one another in love, and being eager to maintain the unity of the Spirit in the bond of peace. And you can see how living other than in these ways would tend to break the unity of the Spirit among God's people. What if some of us acted consistently in a prideful way? How would that damage our unity? Or what if some of us acted without gentleness towards each other? What if some were always forceful or overbearing instead of gentle? How would that affect our unity? Gentleness is one of the many things needed in order for there to be unity and cohesion in the body of Christ. We owe gentleness to each other as we share this calling to be Christ-like people in a self-centered world. Gentle people are eager to maintain unity.

WE ARE CALLED TO OBVIOUS GENTLENESS

While the gentleness of Ephesians four seems to be focused inwardly on other members of the body of Christ, the gentleness of Philippians four seems to face more outwardly toward the whole world.

> *Philippians 4:5 (NKJV) Let your gentle spirit be known to all men. The Lord is near*

Different translations have different words here in verse five. Some English versions say goodness, some gentleness, some (like the ESV) say reasonableness, and some say moderation. What the Bible is saying to us is let these particularly Christian qualities be visible in you. Let all the people who see you know these things about you. Let the qualities of Jesus Christ shine through your lives for the people of the world to see and notice. Have an obvious gentleness about you. Jesus said, "Let your light shine."

The German atheist philosopher Nietzsche once said that if he saw more redeemed people, he might be more inclined to believe in their Redeemer. Christians who do not have changed lives have a credibility problem. If I am trying to tell you how great my dentist is but my teeth are all crooked and in an obvious state of decay, you might not have confidence in his skillset. If I boast about how effective my diet is, while all the while gaining weight, are you likely to want to try that diet? What good does it do to tell others how amazing our savior is if they can't see that we ourselves are being transformed and set free from sin?

LET YOUR LIGHT SHINE

What does Jesus mean by light? Jesus also calls Himself "the light of the world." John calls Him "the life that is the light of men," and, "the light that shines in the darkness" (John 1:4-5).

The light in us is His light, the indwelling Christ, the Holy Spirit within us. The Apostle Paul speaks of "the light of the gospel of the glory of Christ" (II Corinthians 4:4). We have that light shining through our lives if our actions reflect the nature of Jesus Christ; His love, compassion, and gentleness. His light shines through our attitudes, words, and deeds. When people see that our lives have been changed so that we have Jesus' values and see the power of God at work in us, they will agree that we do have a great Savior. When they see redeemed people, they are more inclined to believe that we have a great and true Redeemer. The Christ-like life is the viewing screen on which individual testimony becomes convincing. Why else should we let the good qualities of Jesus Christ be known to all men?

Paul gave Titus a list of important things to teach the people of God. One of the things in his list, of course, was gentleness.

> *Titus 3:1-2   Remind them to be submissive to rulers and authorities, to be obedient, to be ready for every good work, 2 to speak evil of no one, to avoid quarreling, to be gentle, and to show perfect courtesy toward all people.*

Peter taught that gentleness was a very attractive trait for women to have. That gentleness is more attractive in the long run than any physical trait. The long-term impact of having a noticeable gentle and quiet spirit would be quite profound. It would be putting the character of God on display in a way that leads to the transformation of others.

> *I Peter 3:3-4   Do not let your adorning be external—the braiding of hair and the putting on of gold jewelry, or the clothing you wear— 4 but let your adorning be the hidden person of the heart with the imperishable beauty of a gentle and quiet spirit, which in God's sight is very precious.*

GENTLENESS REQUIRED IN CORRECTION

> *II Timothy 2:24-25   And the Lord's servant must not be quarrelsome but kind to everyone, able to teach, patiently enduring evil, 25 correcting his opponents with gentleness. God may perhaps grant them repentance leading to a knowledge of the truth,*

If you have an urge to correct someone, check your demeanor first. Are you inclined at that moment to be gentle or harsh? Are you correcting them because you love them? Are you correcting them to show them how wrong they are? If you are attempting to correct someone, then you ought to be functioning in God's wisdom to do that. And we see in James that God's wisdom is gentle.

> *James 3:17   But the wisdom from above is first pure, then peaceable, gentle, open to reason, full of mercy and good fruits, impartial and sincere.*

THE REWARD AND INHERITANCE OF THE GENTLE

> *Matthew 5:5   Blessed are the meek, for they shall inherit the earth.*

> *Proverbs 15:1   Blessed are the meek, for they shall inherit the earth.*

There is a blessing in store for the gentle people. For those who hold back their right to vengeance and instead wait for God's justice, a great reward is promised. Remember that gentleness or meekness is not weakness, but is power that is under control. We may have the power to get our own revenge in various ways, but the gentle person understands that the Lord has declared that all vengeance is His. The promised reward is amazing. They shall inherit the earth.   This does not mean that the meek will suddenly own everything during this lifetime. Certainly, it is true that the meek will inherit the new earth one day. But I think it also means that there is some reward in the here and now. At the time when man sinned, the earth was cursed.

> *Genesis 3:17-19   And to Adam he said, "Because you have listened to the voice of your wife and have eaten of the tree of which I commanded you, 'You shall not eat of it,' cursed is the ground because of you; in pain you shall eat of it all the days of your life; 18 thorns and thistles it shall bring forth for you: and you shall eat the plants of the field.   19 By the sweat of your face you shall eat bread, till you return to the ground, for out of it you were taken; for you are dust, and to dust you shall return."*

The curse on the earth almost made the earth into an enemy of man. As he tried to make his living from the soil, he would often be defeated and fail. The elements would fight against him. To some degree, perhaps this curse is defeated in the lives of the truly meek. They inherit the earth and find things a little easier going in their personal struggles. God watches over them and provides for them in miraculous ways.

DISCUSSION QUESTIONS:

1 – Do Christians owe gentleness to each other? Why?

2 – Why is it necessary for those who are outside of the body of Christ to see an obvious gentleness in the people of God?

3 – Explain why gentleness is required in the correction of others.

37 WHAT IS SELF-CONTROL?

Galatians 5:22-25   But the fruit of the Spirit is love, joy, peace, patience, kindness, goodness, faithfulness, 23 gentleness, self-control; against such things there is no law. 24 And those who belong to Christ Jesus have crucified the flesh with its passions and desires. 25 If we live by the Spirit, let us also keep in step with the Spirit.

We have now come to the last part of the fruit if the Spirit. The fruit of the Spirit is self-control. What is self-control? To describe self-control in a general way you could say that it is resisting or opposing the impulses of the flesh. It is deliberately not doing what your sinful nature desires to do. It can be anything from saying no to that tempting dessert, to staying out of inappropriate conversations at work or school, to resisting the anger in you that seems to rise up to a boiling point in mere seconds. Self-control is you saying, "no!" to you. It is saying no to the flesh you. It is keeping a restraining control over the beast inside of you. It is getting the victory over the sinful nature. The Bible tells us that self-control is one of the important things that comes to us included in the package with our salvation.

Titus 2:11-12   For the grace of God has appeared, bringing salvation for all people, 12 training us to renounce ungodliness and worldly passions, and to live self-controlled, upright, and godly lives in the present age,

I like how it says that the grace of God has come for more than one reason. The grace of God comes to save us, and to train us. The grace of God comes to help us by training us to renounce ungodliness and worldly passions, and to help us to live self-controlled, upright and godly lives. So, self-control is a gift from God. It is a fruit of the Spirit. It is something that you will find in the life of a true believer. It will not be absent from the true believer, at least not forever, because it is given as a gift from God. And as a gift from God, it will not fail to bloom in the lives if his own people.

But although it is a gift, it is one of those gifts that you have to open up, take out of the box, and put to use yourself (in a way). Like the gift that the promised land was to Israel. They were given the land. It was given from God to them, but they still had to fight for it. They had to exercise some military discipline to take it by force. They had to exert their own wills in a strenuous effort to obtain the gift that they were given. They had to work at the gift. Self-control is one of these kinds of gifts. The gift is not some finished product. It's more like a tool that will enable you to participate with the Holy Spirit in bringing about the finished product.

> I Peter 1:5-10   For this very reason, make every effort to supplement your faith with virtue, and virtue with knowledge, 6 and knowledge with self-control, and self-control with steadfastness, and steadfastness with godliness, 7and godliness with brotherly affection, and brotherly affection with love. 8For if these qualities are yours and are increasing, they keep you from being ineffective or unfruitful in the knowledge of our Lord Jesus Christ. 9For whoever lacks these qualities is so nearsighted that he is blind, having forgotten that he was cleansed from his former sins. 10Therefore, brothers, be all the more diligent to confirm your calling and election, for if you practice these qualities, you will never fall.

Self-control is listed here among the things that we are called upon to put effort towards getting. Verse five, says, make every effort to add these things to your faith. Verse ten says be all the more diligent. We need to put effort into these qualities, including self-control, because if these qualities are yours, if they are in you and if they are increasing, then you will not end up being ineffective or unfruitful in your Christian life. If you have these qualities, including self-control, then the knowledge of Jesus Christ that you have will not be wasted knowledge that leaves you unfruitful. Knowledge without doing is unfruitful knowledge. Faith without works is dead.

It is interesting that in order for us to be effective in our Christian lives, in order for us to be fruitful as we live out our time on earth, these qualities (including self-control) need to be in us, and they also need to be increasing in us. There we see progressive sanctification. In I Peter 5 verse 9, whoever lacks these qualities (including self-control) is so near-sighted that he is blind. He has forgotten that he was cleansed from his former sins. His former sins are not former, because he has not exercised the discipline of self-control to put away the former sins.

The idea of self-control, the essence of self-control, is having a kind of mastery over the self. It is self-rule. It is to rule yourself under the guidance of the Holy Spirit. It is the fruit of a life lived under the authority of the Holy Spirit. You could say that

Self-control is the fruit of discipline, or the fruit of self-discipline. So, my definition of self-control would be this...

> SELF-CONTROL is the God-given ability to restrain oneself, especially in times of provocation or temptation.

But please don't misunderstand me. When I say that self-control is the fruit of self-discipline, I don't mean that you bring about this fruitfulness in yourself or all by yourself. ALL of the fruit of the Spirit is accomplished by the work of the Holy Spirit in you and me, and we can never take credit for accomplishing any of it. You will never see the fruit of the Spirit flourish in your life by simply trying. But, at the same time, you will never see the fruit of the Spirt in your life if you don't try. In other words, our efforts alone will accomplish nothing toward the development of the fruit of the Spirit in our lives. But if we do not exert effort toward the process, it will not happen. It is one of those mysteries that we may not be able to reconcile in our minds with logic. It could be that the idea that the fruit of the Spirit is something which God does in you one hundred percent, but that your cooperation and action are also needed, may not be easy to fully make sense of in our minds. But I think there is a way to help our understanding of this. And I think it would be more accurate for us to say that even the effort which God requires from us is something that God Himself causes to come forth from us. Paul talks about this in His own life.

> *I Corinthians 15:9-10   For I am the least of the apostles, unworthy to be called an apostle, because I persecuted the church of God. 10 But by the grace of God I am what I am, and his grace toward me was not in vain. On the contrary, I worked harder than any of them, though it was not I, but the grace of God that is with me.*

Paul comes into his apostleship in a less prepared condition than the other apostles. He kind of has some catching up to do. And he says "I worked harder than any of them." He added his effort to the growing process. But even that extra, added hard work cannot be credited to Paul himself. He says, "I worked harder than any of them, though it was not I, but the grace of God that is with me." So then, when I tell you that your effort is needed, please understand that it is God who draws that effort out of you and you will never have any credit for what happens in you.

DISCUSSION QUESTIONS:

1 – Can you define self-control in your own words?

2 – Where does the fruit of the Spirit come from?

3 – How can you participate in the cultivation of the fruit of the Spirit in your own life?

38 THE NEED FOR SELF-CONTROL

Proverbs 16:32   Whoever is slow to anger is better than the mighty, and he who rules his spirit than he who takes a city

The person who has self-control is slow to anger, which is better than being mighty. The one who is able to rule his own spirit is better than the one who has the power to conquer a city. Self-control is a greater power than brute force. We need that greater power.

Proverbs 25:28   A man without self-control is like a city broken into and left without walls.

The person who does not have self-control is a vulnerable person. Their life is like a city that has been broken into, invaded by enemies, and left without walls of protection. Self-control is like a wall of protection around your life. It is like a wall of protection around the lives of your family members. If we lack self-control then we, ourselves, are not safe, and no one around us is safe either. Imagine how important a city wall was in the ancient world. Everyone who lived in or near a city depended on the safety which their city wall provided.

> *Romans 7:18-24   For I know that nothing good dwells in me, that is, in my flesh. For I have the desire to do what is right, but not the ability to carry it out. 19 For I do not do the good I want, but the evil I do not want is what I keep on doing. 20 Now if I do what I do not want, it is no longer I who do it, but sin that dwells within me. 21 So I find it to be a law that when I want to do right, evil lies close at hand. 22 For I delight in the law of God, in my inner being, 23 but I see in my members another law waging war against the law of my mind and making me captive to the law of sin that dwells in my members. 24 Wretched man that I am! Who will deliver me from this body of death?*

On your own, you will never develop self-control. You can try, but what will happen will be something far less than success. You will desire to do what is right, but not have the ability to do it. You will want to do good, but find yourself doing wrong anyway. You will delight in the law of God in the inner being, but will fail over and over again in the way of actions. You will find yourself captive to the law of sin, and you will find yourself in a state of despair, wanting desperately to be free from the captivity of sin. "O wretched man that I am!" you will say. On your own, you will never develop the self-control that is the fruit of the Spirit even though you desperately need it, and even though you crave it like crazy. You cannot manufacture it. But it can still be yours.

> *Romans 7:24-25   Wretched man that I am! Who will deliver me from this body of death? 25 Thanks be to God through Jesus Christ our Lord! So then, I myself serve the law of God with my mind, but with my flesh I serve the law of sin.*

DISCUSSION QUESTIONS:

1 – From Proverbs 16:32, how is it that it is better to have self-control than to have the ability to conquer whole cities?

2 – How does the lack of self-control make a person vulnerable?

3 – Why is it impossible for a fallen human being to sincerely exercise self-control over sin?

39 OUR CALL TO SELF CONTROL

Scripture calls us to have this fruit of self-control. Paul spoke often about self-control, calling on a variety of people to exercise it.

THE OVERSEERS OF GOS'S FLOCK ARE CALLED TO HAVE SELF-CONTROL

I Timothy 3:2   Therefore an overseer must be above reproach, the husband of one wife, sober-minded, self-controlled, respectable, hospitable, able to teach

Titus 1:7-8   For an overseer, as God's steward, must be above reproach. He must not be arrogant or quick-tempered or a drunkard or violent or greedy for gain, 8 but hospitable, a lover of good, self-controlled, upright, holy, and disciplined

OLDER MEN ARE CALLED TO HAVE SELF-CONTROL

Titus 2:2   Older men are to be sober-minded, dignified, self-controlled, sound in faith, in love, and in steadfastness.

YOUNGER MEN ARE CALLED TO HAVE SELF-CONTROL

Titus 2:6   Likewise, urge the younger men to be self-controlled.

WOMEN ARE CALLED TO HAVE SELF-CONTROL

I Timothy 2:9   likewise also that women should adorn themselves in respectable apparel, with modesty and self-control, not with braided hair and gold or pearls or costly attire,

So, overseers, old men, young men, and women are all called to have the Spiritual fruit of self-control. That pretty much covers everyone! The calling to this fruit is important and is for our good. In Proverbs we learn, "A man without self-control is like a city broken into and left without walls" (Proverbs 25:28). This is a picture of no safety, no protection. We need to be self-controlled and alert, because the devil, "prowls around like a roaring lion seeking for someone to devour" (I Peter 5:8). We must also remember the benefits of self-control are not merely temporal. As Christians, we exercise self-control not just for short-term goals, but also, to obtain an imperishable crown.

> *I Corinthians 9:25   Every athlete exercises self-control in all things. They do it to receive a perishable wreath, but we an imperishable.*

THE POWER FOR SELF-CONTROL

When unbelievers say they can't control themselves, ultimately, it is the truth, because they do not have the power to do so. But Paul reminds us that grace not only brings salvation to us, but grace also trains us to live self-controlled lives.

> *II Timothy 1:7   for God gave us a spirit not of fear but of power and love and self-control.*

This means the ability to control oneself comes from the Holy Spirit. As we live in Him and walk with Him and keep in step with Him, this gift of self-control ought to be growing and increasing in us. The Apostle Peter agrees, reminding us that it is God's power that has granted to us all things that pertain to life and godliness, and he calls us to make every effort to live self-controlled lives.

> *II Peter 1:3-6   His divine power has granted to us all things that pertain to life and godliness, through the knowledge of him who called us to his own glory and excellence, 4 by which he has granted to us his precious and very great promises, so that through them you may become partakers of the divine nature, having escaped from the corruption that is in the world because of sinful desire. 5 For this very reason, make every effort to supplement your faith with virtue, and virtue with knowledge, 6 and knowledge with self-control, and self-control with steadfastness, and steadfastness with godliness,*

Thank God we are not left on our own in our temptations. God is faithful. He does not allow us to be tempted beyond our ability to endure, and he also provides a way out.

> *I Corinthians 10:13   No temptation has overtaken you that is not common to man. God is faithful, and he will not let you be tempted beyond your ability, but with the temptation he will also provide the way of escape, that you may be able to endure it.*

With the help then of the Spirit's power working in us, the same power that raised Christ from the dead, let's put every effort into obtaining this fruit of self-control. And what is the great secret of self-control? As far as our part in this goes?

> *Galatians 5:24   And those who belong to Christ Jesus have crucified the flesh with its passions and desires*

Jesus said, "if you want to be my disciple, take up your cross daily and follow me." It is a battle. But it is a battle in which we have been given a decided edge. We have been empowered by the indwelling Holy Spirit to make increasing progress in our fight against the sins that formerly so easily beset us.

> *Galatians 5:16-18   But I say, walk by the Spirit, and you will not gratify the desires of the flesh. 17 For the desires of the flesh are against the Spirit, and the desires of the Spirit are against the flesh, for these are opposed to each other, to keep you from doing the things you want to do. 18 But if you are led by the Spirit, you are not under the law.*

It is a daily battle, a daily struggle, but those in Christ have undergone a fundamental change.

At the moment of salvation, a kind of forever sanctification takes place. An immediate change happens in our basic nature which enables us to have victories over sin which were not possible before. This is followed by a more progressive and active sanctification, as we win one battle after another over the years.

> *Romans 6:12-14   Let not sin therefore reign in your mortal body, to make you obey its passions. 13 Do not present your members to sin as instruments for unrighteousness, but present yourselves to God as those who have been brought from death to life, and your members to God as instruments for righteousness. 14 For sin will have no dominion over you, since you are not under law but under grace.*

For those of us who are born again; who can say that we know that we know the Lord, there is an added strength given to us to overcome sin. And as we walk in the Spirit, we will gain experiential victories. And as believers we certainly enjoy freedom from the "condemnation" of sin.

> *Romans 8:1-2   There is therefore now no condemnation for those who are in Christ Jesus. 2 For the law of the Spirit of life has set you free in Christ Jesus from the law of sin and death.*

It is great news that we are free from the condemnation of sin. But there is more. We are also granted freedom from the "power" of sin. We are given freedom from "the law of sin and death." The "law of the Spirit of life in Christ" provides this freedom! The Holy Spirit helps us to overcome sin in real life.

WHAT THEN IS OUR RESPONSIBILITY?

First of all, our responsibility is to believe that what God's word says about these things is true. Trust in God's Word, that by His grace, our old man of sin was indeed crucified with Christ.

> *Romans 6:6   We know that our old self was crucified with him in order that the body of sin might be brought to nothing, so that we would no longer be enslaved to sin.*

Trust in the fact that God has given us the added strength we need to continue to be people who crucify the flesh.

> *Galatians 5:24   And those who belong to Christ Jesus have crucified the flesh with its passions and desires.*

And then, with such faith and with such God-given strength, continue the process which God began in us. Put to death the deeds of the body (Romans 8:13). Put to death our members here on the earth (Colossians 3:5,8-9). Put ON the new man (Ephesians 4:24). Put on Christ (Galatians 3:27). And even though you know it doesn't depend on you, work as though it all depends on you.

> *Philippians 2:12-13   Therefore, my beloved, as you have always obeyed, so now, not only as in my presence but much more in my absence, work out your own salvation with fear and trembling, 13 for it is God who works in you, both to will and to work for his good pleasure.*

And remember that you are not alone, that God is at work in you too! So, how do we get to the place where the grace of God moves upon us to make us work hard at these things like He made Paul work harder? How do we get to the place where God works in us not only to will, but to do also? Well, I hope that is happening right now. This is at least one of the ways that God moves on us to do, and to exert effort, and to be diligent. It is during the preaching and the teaching of God's word when we are moved to work toward making our calling and election sure. It is as we encounter the written or preached word of God that we are compelled to strive toward working out our own salvation with fear and trembling. It is during the teaching and preaching of the word, during the studying of God's word, where that holy impetus hits us and propels us into action.

DISCUSSION QUESTIONS:

1 – What are some of the benefits of having the fruit of self-control?

2 – Why is self-control not obtainable by the self alone?

3 – What stirs us up to desire and fight for self-control?

40 SPECIFIC AREAS WHERE CHRISTIANS NEED SELF-CONTROL

I Corinthians 6:12   "All things are lawful for me," but not all things are helpful. "All things are lawful for me," but I will not be dominated by anything.

There are, of course, many different areas in our lives where self-control is needed. Interestingly, not all of them are blatantly or obviously sinful. Even many things which are lawful for us may be things which we indulge in, in an unhealthy, unwise or unloving way. So some of the areas we will briefly discuss will be clearly sinful things, but others will come under the umbrella of things which could master or dominate us, but are not in themselves loudly sinful.

1 SELF-CONTROL IS NEEDED IN OUR THOUGHT-LIFE

> *Philippians 4:8   Finally, brothers, whatever is true, whatever is honorable, whatever is just, whatever is pure, whatever is lovely, whatever is commendable, if there is any excellence, if there is anything worthy of praise, think about these things*

Thinking is like practicing actions. If you allow an idea to bounce around in your mind, if you turn it over and over and consider it from every aspect and from every angle, and you dwell upon it, then it becomes easier to actually do it. It is as though the thoughts lay down the concrete roads upon which the car of action proceeds. The thoughts lay the wires which conduct the electricity of actions. Thinking in the right way is like rehearsing for a play; you learn your lines, you practice, and when it is time to act, then you are much more prepared. When you have thought a thing over and over, and then you come to the time of action, you know just what to do because you are prepared. It is of the utmost importance therefore that you be careful what you think, because thought is the precursor of action. Thought is the practice of action. So, if you are thinking a lot of bad things then you will end up doing some of them. As a man thinks in his heart, so is he (Proverbs 23:7). As you think, so you are, almost without knowing it.

> *Proverbs 4:23*   *Keep your heart with all diligence, for out of it spring the issues of life.*

If a person indulges in ungodly thoughts he will almost involuntarily deteriorate into ungodliness. He cannot help it. There is a profound passage in Romans 1:1-32, where it says that because they refused to retain God in their minds but cherished their vile lusts in their thoughts, God gave them up to their own passions to defile themselves.

> *Romans 1:21*   *because, although they knew God, they did not glorify Him as God, nor were thankful, but became futile in their thoughts, and their foolish hearts were darkened*

They became foolish in their thoughts and this caused their hearts to darken. So, you see, bad thoughts created bad character. There is a direct relationship between the ugly thinking and the resultant ugly character.

> *Romans 1:24-25   Therefore God also gave them up to uncleanness, in the lusts of their hearts, to dishonor their bodies among themselves, 25 who exchanged the truth of God for the lie, and worshiped and served the creature rather than the Creator, who is blessed forever. Amen.*

> *Romans 1:28   And even as they did not like to retain God in their knowledge, God gave them over to a debased mind, to do those things which are not fitting*

Notice the progression; in verse twenty-one they became futile in their thoughts, and their hearts were darkened. Then in verses twenty-four and twenty-five God gave them up to their own way of thinking. Because of the content of their thoughts, they were losing godliness and gaining vileness. And by verse twenty-eight the thoughts had become actions and had fixed their character in a negative way. If a man is habitually cherishing unholy, impure, and untrue thoughts, he will become an unholy, impure, and untrue man. Our character takes on the nature of our inward thinking. If a man is always thinking kind thoughts, he will be reflexively kind. If he is generous in his thought, he will be generous in his actions. If he is loving and tender in his thoughts, he will be loving and tender in his behavior. Our thoughts are like sewing machines in our heads, constantly at work creating the clothing which our character will wear. If you will care for your thoughts, then the thoughts will mold your character in a positive way.

2 SELF-CCONTROL IS NEEDED OVER THE TONGUE

> *James 3:2-10   For we all stumble in many ways. And if anyone does not stumble in what he says, he is a perfect man, able also to bridle his whole body. 3 If we put bits into the mouths of horses so that they obey us, we guide their whole bodies as well. 4 Look at the ships also: though they are so large and are driven by strong winds, they are guided by a very small rudder wherever the will of the pilot directs. 5 So also the tongue is a small member, yet it boasts of great things. How great a forest is set ablaze by such a small fire! 6 And the tongue is a fire, a world of unrighteousness. The tongue is set among our members, staining the whole body, setting on fire the entire course of life, and set on fire by hell. 7 For every kind of beast and bird, of reptile and sea creature, can be tamed and has been tamed by mankind, 8 but no human being can tame the tongue. It is a restless evil, full of deadly poison. 9 With it we bless our Lord and Father, and with it we curse people who are made in the likeness of God. 10 From the same mouth come*

blessing and cursing. My brothers, these things ought not to be so.

How many of us have ever said something which we regret saying? Look at the powerful things James says about the human tongue. It takes a perfect person to control their own mouth. Our words set forests on fire. The tongue is a world of unrighteousness. It can set on fire the entire course of life. The tongue can stain the whole body. No human being is able to tame his own tongue. Blessings come out of the mouth, but curses do too.

3 SELF-CONTROL IS NEEDED OVER APPETITES

Proverbs 23:1-2   When you sit down to eat with a ruler, observe carefully what is before you, 2 and put a knife to your throat if you are given to appetite.

In this situation, sitting down at a meal with a ruler, why do you think you should put a knife to your throat if you are given to appetite? Because you are in a particularly dangerous place for you. If you are given to appetites, if the presented delicacies are something you are vulnerable to, be careful. Watch out because it's a trap. And if you fall for the trap, you may be about to be owned. You

286

may be about to be brought under the power of the thing, and be returned to your slavery to sin.

> *Philippians 3:18-19   For many, of whom I have often told you and now tell you even with tears, walk as enemies of the cross of Christ. 19 Their end is destruction, their god is their belly, and they glory in their shame, with minds set on earthly things.*

Every kind of sensuality, every kind of appetite, when indulged in, becomes something which is opposed to the cross in your life. If you give in to temptations – whether food, sex, drugs, drink, entertainment – you are doing the opposite of letting the cross be applied in your life. I want to be careful about being legalistic here. All things are lawful for us, but not all things are healthy for all of us. You may find yourself interested in something that is perfectly lawful and is not blatantly sinful. Maybe a hobby, maybe a sport, maybe a career. And as that thing of great interest to you grows larger and larger in its ability to grab your attention, you may begin to lose some of your interest in the things of God. It is like the soil of Mark where the seed of the word is sown among the thorns (Mark 4:18-19). The word seems to flourish in the soil, but eventually the thorns, which the Lord says represent "the cares of this world," choke out the word and it becomes unfruitful in this person's life.

4 SELF-CONTROL IS NEEDED OVER SEXUAL DESIRE

> *I Corinthians 7:1-5   Now concerning the matters about which you   wrote: "It is good for a man not to have sexual relations with a woman." 2 But because of the temptation to sexual immorality, each man should have his own wife and each woman her own husband. 3 The husband should give to his wife her conjugal rights, and likewise the wife to her husband. 4 For the wife does not have authority over her own body, but the husband does. Likewise, the husband does not have authority over his own body, but the wife does. 5 Do not deprive one another, except perhaps by agreement for a limited time, that you may devote yourselves to prayer; but then come together again, so that Satan may not tempt you because of your lack of self-control.*

The physical union of a husband and wife is honorable and blessed of God. In I Corinthians chapter seven, the apostle Paul gives instruction for the proper control of sexual desire within marriage. He goes on to say later, in verses eight and nine, that if the unmarried and widows "cannot exercise self-control, they should marry, for it is better to marry than to burn with passion."

People who remain unmarried need the "self-control" of the Holy Spirit to control normal sexual desires. The importance of this control is made clear in...

> *I Thessalonians 4:3-7   For this is the will of God, your sanctification: that you abstain from sexual immorality; 4 that each one of you know how to control his own body in holiness and honor, 5 not in the passion of lust like the Gentiles who do not know God; 6 that no one transgress and wrong his brother in this matter, because the Lord is an avenger in all these things, as we told you beforehand and solemnly warned you. 7 For God has not called us for impurity, but in holiness.*

To abstain from sexual immorality is the will of God for us. What is included in sexual immorality? Any sexual activity that takes place outside of the marriage of one man to one woman is sexual immorality. So if the need to have sex overwhelms the single person, then they need to marry in order to stay withing the boundaries of God's sexual rules.

Is it possible for there to be sexual immorality inside of the marriage of one man to one woman? Yes, it is possible. There can be unfaithfulness, or indulgence in pornography. There can be harmful behavior in which abuse or force are used. The withholding of sexual activity can also be a kind of sexual immorality as Paul describes in I Corinthians 7:5.

Self-control is an essential part of the Christian life, and we should be grateful that the Lord implants His ability in us to bring about self-control in the various ways that we truly need it.

DISCUSSION QUESTIONS:

1 – Explain why it is important to have self-control in your thought life.

2 – Describe how self-control over the tongue has either rescued you from a difficult situation - or how the lack of self-control over the tongue has gotten you into trouble.

3 – How much does the lack of self-control over sexual desires and other appetites cause societal problems? Give examples.

BOOKS BY THIS AUTHOR

God Is Speaking 1 (Father, Son & Holy Spirit

God Is Speaking 2 (The Bible, Prophets & Preachers

God Is Speaking 3 (Visions, Dreams & Voices)

God Is Speaking (Complete Series In One Volume)

Perilous Times: The Degrading Character Of The Last Days

Hungering For God

Lessons From Philippians: The Christian Struggle For Authenticity And Joy

The Secret To Finding Your Godly Husband: A Biblical Approach To Marriage

The Secret To Finding Your God-Given Wife: A Biblical Approach To Marriage

The Secret To Finding Your Christian Spouse: A Biblical Approach To Marriage

Combines the two marriage books in one.

Printed in Great Britain
by Amazon